D1398815

GRAPHYCO BOOKS

Published by Graphyco Editions

CONTENT

CHAPTER I

"A Revelation of Love—in Sixteen Shewings"

This is a Revelation of Love that Jesus Christ, our endless bliss, made in Sixteen Shewings, or Revelations particular.

Of the which the First is of His precious crowning with thorns; and therewith was comprehended and specified the Trinity, with the Incarnation, and unity betwixt God and man's soul; with many fair shewings of endless wisdom and teachings of love: in which all the Shewings that follow be grounded and oned.

The Second is the changing of colour of His fair face in token of His dearworthy Passion.

The Third is that our Lord God, Allmighty Wisdom, All-Love, right as verily as He hath made everything that is, all-so verily He doeth and worketh all-thing that is done.

The Fourth is the scourging of His tender body, with plenteous shedding of His blood.

The Fifth is that the Fiend is overcome by the precious Passion of Christ.

The Sixth is the worshipful thanking by our Lord God in which He rewardeth His blessed servants in Heaven.

The Seventh is [our] often feeling of weal and woe; (the feeling of weal is gracious touching and lightening, with true assuredness of endless joy; the feeling of woe is temptation by heaviness and irksomeness of our fleshly living;) with ghostly understanding that we are kept all as securely in Love in woe as in weal, by the Goodness of God.

The Eighth is of the last pains of Christ, and His cruel dying.

The Ninth is of the pleasing which is in the Blissful Trinity by the hard Passion of Christ and His rueful dying: in which joy and pleasing He willeth that we be solaced and mirthed with Him, till when we come to the fulness in Heaven.

The Tenth is, our Lord Jesus sheweth in love His blissful heart even cloven in two, rejoicing.

The Eleventh is an high ghostly Shewing of His dearworthy Mother.

The Twelfth is that our Lord is most worthy Being.

The Thirteenth is that our Lord God willeth we have great regard to all the deeds that He hath done: in the great nobleness of the making of all things; and the excellency of man's making, which is above all his works; and the precious Amends that He hath made for man's sin, turning all our blame into endless worship. In which Shewing also our Lord saith: *Behold and see! For by the same Might, Wisdom, and Goodness that I have done all this, by the same Might, Wisdom, and Goodness I shall make well all that is not well; and thou shalt see it.* And in this He willeth that we keep us in the Faith and truth of Holy Church, not desiring to see into His secret things now, save as it belongeth to us in this life.

The Fourteenth is that our Lord is the Ground of our Prayer. Herein were seen two properties: the one is rightful prayer, the other is steadfast trust; which He willeth should both be alike large; and thus our prayer pleaseth Him and He of His Goodness fulfilleth it.

The Fifteenth is that we shall suddenly be taken from all our pain and from all our woe, and of His Goodness we shall come up above, where we shall have our Lord Jesus for our meed and be fulfilled with joy and bliss in Heaven.

The Sixteenth is that the Blissful Trinity, our Maker, in Christ Jesus our Saviour endlessly dwelleth in our soul, worshipfully ruling and protecting all things, us mightily and wisely saving and keeping, for love; and we shall not be overcome of our Enemy.

CHAPTER II

"A simple creature unlettered.—Which creature afore desired three
gifts of God"

These Revelations were shewed to a simple creature unlettered, the
year of our Lord 1373, the Thirteenth day of May. Which creature
[had] afore desired three gifts of God. The First was mind of His
Passion; the Second was bodily sickness in youth, at thirty years of
age; the Third was to have of God's gift three wounds.

As to the First, methought I had some feeling in the Passion of Christ,
but yet I desired more by the grace of God. Methought I would have
been that time with Mary Magdalene, and with other that were
Christ's lovers, and therefore I desired a bodily sight wherein I might
have more knowledge of the bodily pains of our Saviour and of the
compassion of our Lady and of all His true lovers that saw, that time,
His pains. For I would be one of them and suffer with Him. Other sight
nor shewing of God desired I never none, till the soul were disparted
from the body. The cause of this petition was that after the shewing I
should have the more true mind in the Passion of Christ.

The Second came to my mind with contrition; [I] freely desiring that
sickness [to be] so hard as to death, that I might in that sickness
receive all my rites of Holy Church, myself thinking that I should die,
and that all creatures might suppose the same that saw me: for I would
have no manner of comfort of earthly life. In this sickness I desired to
have all manner of pains bodily and ghostly that I should have if I
should die, (with all the dreads and tempests of the fiends) except the
outpassing of the soul. And this I meant for [that] I would be purged,
by the mercy of God, and afterward live more to the worship of God
because of that sickness. And that for the more furthering in my death:
for I desired to be soon with my God.

These two desires of the Passion and the sickness I desired with a
condition, saying thus: *Lord, Thou knowest what I would,—if it be
Thy will that I have it—; and if it be not Thy will, good Lord, be not
displeased: for I will nought but as Thou wilt.*

For the Third [petition], by the grace of God and teaching of Holy
Church I conceived a mighty desire to receive three wounds in my

life: that is to say, the wound of very contrition, the wound of kind compassion, and the wound of steadfast longing toward God. And all this last petition I asked without any condition.

These two desires aforesaid passed from my mind, but the third dwelled with me continually.

CHAPTER III

"I desired to suffer with Him"

And when I was thirty years old and a half, God sent me a bodily sickness, in which I lay three days and three nights; and on the fourth night I took all my rites of Holy Church, and weened not to have lived till day. And after this I languored forth two days and two nights, and on the third night I weened oftentimes to have passed; and so weened they that were with me.

And being in youth as yet, I thought it great sorrow to die;—but for nothing that was in earth that meliked to live for, nor for no pain that I had fear of: for I trusted in God of His mercy. But it was to have lived that I might have loved God better, and longer time, that I might have the more knowing and loving of God in bliss of Heaven. For methought all the time that I had lived here so little and so short in regard of that endless bliss,—I thought [it was as] nothing. Wherefore I thought: *Good Lord, may my living no longer be to Thy worship!* And I understood by my reason and by my feeling of my pains that I should die; and I assented fully with all the will of my heart to be at God's will.

Thus I dured till day, and by then my body was dead from the middle downwards, as to my feeling. Then was I minded to be set upright, backward leaning, with help,—for to have more freedom of my heart to be at God's will, and thinking on God while my life would last.

My Curate was sent for to be at my ending, and by that time when he came I had set my eyes, and might not speak. He set the Cross before my face and said: *I have brought thee the Image of thy Maker and Saviour: look thereupon and comfort thee therewith.*

Methought I was well [as it was], for my eyes were set uprightward unto Heaven, where I trusted to come by the mercy of God; but nevertheless I assented to set my eyes on the face of the Crucifix, if I might; and so I did. For methought I might longer dure to look even-forth than right up.

After this my sight began to fail, and it was all dark about me in the chamber, as if it had been night, save in the Image of the Cross whereon I beheld a common light; and I wist not how. All that was away from the Cross was of horror to me, as if it had been greatly occupied by the fiends.

After this the upper part of my body began to die, so far forth that scarcely I had any feeling;—with shortness of breath. And then I weened in sooth to have passed.

And in this [moment] suddenly all my pain was taken from me, and I was as whole (and specially in the upper part of my body) as ever I was afore.

I marvelled at this sudden change; for methought it was a privy working of God, and not of nature. And yet by the feeling of this ease I trusted never the more to live; nor was the feeling of this ease any full ease unto me: for methought I had liefer have been delivered from this world.

Then came suddenly to my mind that I should desire the second wound of our Lord's gracious gift: that my body might be fulfilled with mind and feeling of His blessed Passion. For I would that His pains were my pains, with compassion and afterward longing to God. But in this I desired never bodily sight nor shewing of God, but compassion such as a kind soul might have with our Lord Jesus, that for love would be a mortal man: and therefore I desired to suffer with Him.

THE FIRST REVELATION

CHAPTER IV

"I saw ... as it were in the time of His Passion.... And in the same
Shewing suddenly the Trinity filled my heart with utmost joy"

In this [moment] suddenly I saw the red blood trickle down from
under the Garland hot and freshly and right plenteously, as it were in
the time of His Passion when the Garland of thorns was pressed on
His blessed head who was both God and Man, the same that suffered
thus for me. I conceived truly and mightily that it was Himself shewed
it me, without any mean.

And in the same Shewing suddenly the Trinity fulfilled my heart most
of joy. And so I understood it shall be in heaven without end to all that
shall come there. For the Trinity is God: God is the Trinity; the Trinity
is our Maker and Keeper, the Trinity is our everlasting love and
everlasting joy and bliss, by our Lord Jesus Christ. And this was
shewed in the First [Shewing] and in all: for where Jesus appeareth,
the blessed Trinity is understood, as to my sight.

And I said: *Benedicite Domine!* This I said for reverence in my
meaning, with mighty voice; and full greatly was astonied for wonder
and marvel that I had, that He that is so reverend and dreadful will be
so homely with a sinful creature living in wretched flesh.

This [Shewing] I took for the time of my temptation,—for methought
by the sufferance of God I should be tempted of fiends ere I died.
Through this sight of the blessed Passion, with the Godhead that I saw
in mine understanding, I knew well that *It* was strength enough for me,
yea, and for all creatures living, against all the fiends of hell and
ghostly temptation.

In this [Shewing] He brought our blessed Lady to my understanding. I
saw her ghostly, in bodily likeness: a simple maid and a meek, young
of age and little waxen above a child, in the stature that she was when
she conceived. Also God shewed in part the wisdom and the truth of
her soul: wherein I understood the reverent beholding in which she
beheld her God and Maker, marvelling with great reverence that He
would be born of her that was a simple creature of His making. And

this wisdom and truth: knowing the greatness of her Maker and the littleness of herself that was made,—caused her to say full meekly to Gabriel: *Lo me, God's handmaid!* In this sight I understood soothly that she is more than all that God made beneath her in worthiness and grace; for above her is nothing that is made but the blessed [Manhood] of Christ, as to my sight.

CHAPTER V

"God, of Thy Goodness, give me Thyself;—only in Thee I have all"

In this same time our Lord shewed me a spiritual sight of His homely loving.

I saw that He is to us everything that is good and comfortable for us: He is our clothing that for love wrappeth us, claspeth us, and all encloseth us for tender love, that He may never leave us; being to us all-thing that is good, as to mine understanding.

Also in this He shewed me a little thing, the quantity of an hazel-nut, in the palm of my hand; and it was as round as a ball. I looked thereupon with eye of my understanding, and thought: *What may this be?* And it was answered generally thus: *it is all that is made.* I marvelled how it might last, for methought it might suddenly have fallen to naught for little[ness]. And I was answered in my understanding: *It lasteth, and ever shall [last] for that God loveth it.* And so All-thing hath the Being by the love of God.

In this Little Thing I saw three properties. The first is that God made it, the second is that God loveth it, the third, that God keepeth it. But what is to me verily the Maker, the Keeper, and the Lover,—I cannot tell; for till I am Substantially oned to Him, I may never have full rest nor very bliss: that is to say, till I be so fastened to Him, that there is right nought that is made betwixt my God and me.

It needeth us to have knowing of the littleness of creatures and to hold as nought all-thing that is made, for to love and have God that is unmade. For this is the cause why we be not all in ease of heart and soul: that we seek here rest in those things that are so little, wherein is no rest, and know not our God that is All-mighty, All-wise, All-good. For He is the Very Rest. God willeth to be known, and it pleaseth Him that we rest in Him; for all that is beneath Him sufficeth not us. And this is the cause why that no soul is rested till it is made nought as to all things that are made. When it is willingly made nought, for love, to have Him that is all, then is it able to receive spiritual rest.

Also our Lord God shewed that it is full great pleasance to Him that a helpless soul come to Him simply and plainly and homely. For this is the natural yearnings of the soul, by the touching of the Holy Ghost (as by the understanding that I have in this Shewing): *God, of Thy Goodness, give me Thyself: for Thou art enough to me, and I may nothing ask that is less that may be full worship to Thee; and if I ask anything that is less, ever me wanteth,—but only in Thee I have all.*

And these words are full lovely to the soul, and full near touch they the will of God and His Goodness. For His Goodness comprehendeth all His creatures and all His blessed works, and overpasseth without end. For He is the endlessness, and He hath made us only to Himself, and restored us by His blessed Passion, and keepeth us in His blessed love; and all this of His Goodness.

CHAPTER VI

"The Goodness of God is the highest prayer, and it cometh down to the lowest part of our need"

This Shewing was made to learn our soul wisely to cleave to the Goodness of God.

And in that time the custom of our praying was brought to mind: how we use for lack of understanding and knowing of Love, to take many means [whereby to beseech Him].

Then saw I truly that it is more worship to God, and more very delight, that we faithfully pray to Himself of His Goodness and cleave thereunto by His Grace, with true understanding, and steadfast by love, than if we took all the means that heart can think. For if we took all these means, it is too little, and not full worship to God: but in His Goodness is all the whole, and *there* faileth right nought.

For this, as I shall tell, came to my mind in the same time: We pray to God for [the sake of] His holy flesh and His precious blood, His holy

Passion, His dearworthy death and wounds: and all the blessed kindness, the endless life that we have of all this, is His Goodness. And we pray Him for [the sake of] His sweet Mother's love that Him bare; and all the help we have of her is of His Goodness. And we pray by His holy Cross that he died on, and all the virtue and the help that we have of the Cross, it is of His Goodness. And on the same wise, all the help that we have of special saints and all the blessed Company of Heaven, the dearworthy love and endless friendship that we have of them, it is of His Goodness. For God of His Goodness hath ordained means to help us, full fair and many: of which the chief and principal mean is the blessed nature that He took of the Maid, with all the means that go afore and come after which belong to our redemption and to endless salvation. Wherefore it pleaseth Him that we seek Him and worship through means, understanding that He is the Goodness of all.

For the Goodness of God is the highest prayer, and it cometh down to the lowest part of our need. It quickeneth our soul and bringeth it on life, and maketh it for to waxen in grace and virtue. It is nearest in nature; and readiest in grace: for *it* is the same grace that the soul seeketh, and ever shall seek till we know verily that He hath us all in Himself enclosed.

For He hath no despite of that He hath made, nor hath He any disdain to serve us at the simplest office that to our body belongeth in nature, for love of the soul that He hath made to His own likeness.

For as the body is clad in the cloth, and the flesh in the skin, and the bones in the flesh, and the heart in the whole, so are we, soul and body, clad in the Goodness of God, and enclosed. Yea, and more homely: for all these may waste and wear away, but the Goodness of God is ever whole; and more near to us, without any likeness; for truly our Lover desireth that our soul cleave to Him with all its might, and that we be ever-more cleaving to His Goodness. For of all things that heart may think, this pleaseth most God, and soonest speedeth [the soul].

For our soul is so specially loved of Him that is highest, that it overpasseth the knowing of all creatures: that is to say, there is no creature that is made that may [fully] know how much and how sweetly and how tenderly our Maker loveth us. And therefore we may with grace and His help stand in spiritual beholding, with everlasting marvel of this high, overpassing, inestimable Love that Almighty God hath to us of His Goodness. And therefore we may ask of our Lover with reverence all that we will.

For our natural Will is to have God, and the Good Will of God is to have us; and we may never cease from willing nor from longing till we have Him in fullness of joy: and then may we no more desire.

For He willeth that we be occupied in knowing and loving till the time that we shall be fulfilled in Heaven; and therefore was this lesson of Love shewed, with all that followeth, as ye shall see. For the strength and the Ground of all was shewed in the First Sight. For of all things the beholding and the loving of the Maker maketh the soul to seem less in his own sight, and most filleth him with reverent dread and true meekness; with plenty of charity to his even-Christians.

CHAPTER VII

"The Shewing is not other than of faith, nor less nor more"

And [it was] to learn us this, as to mine understanding, [that] our Lord God shewed our Lady Saint Mary in the same time: that is to say, the high Wisdom and Truth *she* had in beholding of her Maker so great, so holy, so mighty, and so good. This greatness and this nobleness of the beholding of God fulfilled her with reverent dread, and withal she saw herself so little and so low, so simple and so poor, in regard of her Lord God, that this reverent dread fulfilled her with meekness. And thus, by this ground [of meekness] she was fulfilled with grace and with all manner of virtues, and overpasseth all creatures.

In all the time that He shewed this that I have told now in spiritual sight, I saw the bodily sight lasting of the plenteous bleeding of the Head. The great drops of blood fell down from under the Garland like pellots, seeming as it had come out of the veins; and in the coming out they were brown-red, for the blood was full thick; and in the spreading-abroad they were bright-red; and when they came to the brows, then they vanished; notwithstanding, the bleeding continued till many things were seen and understood. The fairness and the lifelikeness is like nothing but the same; the plenteousness is like to the drops of water that fall off the eaves after a great shower of rain, that fall so thick that no man may number them with bodily wit; and for the roundness, they were like to the scale of herring, in the spreading on the forehead. These three came to my mind in the time: pellots, for roundness, in the coming out of the blood; the scale of herring, in the spreading in the forehead, for roundness; the drops off eaves, for the plenteousness innumerable.

This Shewing was quick and life-like, and horrifying and dreadful, sweet and lovely. And of all the sight it was most comfort to me that our God and Lord that is so reverend and dreadful, is so homely and courteous: and this most fulfilled me with comfort and assuredness of soul.

And to the understanding of this He shewed this open example:—

It is the most worship that a solemn King or a great Lord may do a poor servant if he will be homely with him, and specially if he sheweth it *himself*, of a full true meaning, and with a glad cheer, both privately and in company. Then thinketh this poor creature thus: *And what might this noble Lord do of more worship and joy to me than to shew me that am so simple this marvellous homeliness? Soothly it is more joy and pleasance to me than [if] he gave me great gifts and were himself strange in manner.*

This bodily example was shewed so highly that man's heart might be ravished and almost forgetting itself for joy of the great homeliness. Thus it fareth with our Lord Jesus and with us. For verily it is the most joy that may be, as to my sight, that He that is highest and mightiest, noblest and worthiest, is lowest and meekest, homeliest and most courteous: and truly and verily this marvellous joy shall be shewn us all when we see Him.

And this willeth our Lord that we seek for and trust to, joy and delight in, comforting us and solacing us, as we may with His grace and with His help, unto the time that we see it verily. For the most fulness of joy that we shall have, as to my sight, is the marvellous courtesy and homeliness of our Father, that is our Maker, in our Lord Jesus Christ that is our Brother and our Saviour.

But this marvellous homeliness may no man fully see in this time of life, save he have it of special shewing of our Lord, or of great plenty of grace inwardly given of the Holy Ghost. But faith and belief with charity deserveth the meed: and so it is had, by grace; for in faith, with hope and charity, our life is grounded. The Shewing, made to whom that God will, plainly teacheth the same, opened and declared, with many privy points belonging to our Faith which be worshipful to know. And when the Shewing which is given in a time is passed and hid, then the faith keepeth [it] by grace of the Holy Ghost unto our life's end. And thus through the Shewing it is not other than of faith, nor less nor more; as it may be seen in our Lord's teaching in the same matter, by that time that it shall come to the end.

CHAPTER VIII

"In all this I was greatly stirred in charity to my fellow-Christians that they might see and know the same that I saw"

And as long as I saw this sight of the plenteous bleeding of the Head I might never cease from these words: *Benedicite Domine!*

In which Shewing I understood six things:—The first is, the tokens of the blessed Passion and the plenteous shedding of His precious blood. The second is, the Maiden that is His dearworthy Mother. The third is, the blissful Godhead that ever was, is, and ever shall be: Almighty, All-Wisdom, All-Love. The fourth is, all-thing that He hath made.— For well I wot that heaven and earth and all that is made is great and large, fair and good; but the cause why it shewed so little to my sight was for that I saw it in the presence of Him that is the Maker of all things: for to a soul that seeth the Maker of all, all that is made seemeth full little.—The fifth is: He that made all things for love, by the same love keepeth them, and shall keep them without end. The sixth is, that God is all that is good, as to my sight, and the goodness that each thing hath, it is He.

And all these our Lord shewed me in the first Sight, with time and space to behold it. And the bodily sight stinted, but the spiritual sight dwelled in mine understanding, and I abode with reverent dread, joying in that I saw. And I desired, as I durst, to see more, if it were His will, or else [to see for] longer time the same.

In all this I was greatly stirred in charity to mine even-Christians, that they might see and know the same that I saw: for I would it were comfort to them. For all this Sight was shewed [with] general [regard]. Then said I to them that were about me: *It is to-day Doomsday with me*. And this I said for that I thought to have died. (For that day that a man dieth, he is judged as shall be without end, as to mine understanding.) This I said for that I would they might love God the better, for to make them to have in mind that this life is short, as they might see in example. For in all this time I weened to have died; and that was marvel to me, and troublous partly: for methought this Vision was shewed for them that should live. And that which I say of me, I say in the person of all mine even-Christians: for I am taught in the Spiritual Shewing of our Lord God that He meaneth so. And therefore I pray you all for God's sake, and counsel you for your own profit, that ye leave the beholding of a poor creature that it was shewed to, and mightily, wisely, and meekly behold God that of His courteous love and endless goodness would shew it generally, in comfort of us all. For it is God's will that ye take it with great joy and pleasance, as if Jesus had shewed it to you all.

CHAPTER IX

"If I look singularly to myself, I am right nought"

Because of the Shewing I am not good but if I love God the better: and in as much as ye love God the better, it is more to you than to me. I say not this to them that be wise, for they wot it well; but I say it to you that be simple, for ease and comfort: for we are all one in comfort. For truly it was not shewed me that God loved me better than the least soul that is in grace; for I am certain that there be many that never had Shewing nor sight but of the common teaching of Holy Church, that love God better than I. For if I look singularly to myself, I am right nought; but in [the] general [Body] I am, I hope, in oneness of charity with all mine even-Christians.

For in this oneness standeth the life of all mankind that shall be saved. For God is all that is good, as to my sight, and God hath made all that is made, and God loveth all that He hath made: and he that loveth generally all his even-Christians for God, he loveth all that is. For in mankind that shall be saved is comprehended all: that is to say, all that is made and the Maker of all. For in man is God, and God is in all. And I hope by the grace of God he that beholdeth it thus shall be truly taught and mightily comforted, if he needeth comfort.

I speak of them that shall be saved, for in this time God shewed me none other. But in all things I believe as Holy Church believeth, preacheth, and teacheth. For the Faith of Holy Church, the which I had aforehand understood and, as I hope, by the grace of God earnestly kept in use and custom, stood continually in my sight: [I] willing and meaning never to receive anything that might be contrary thereunto. And with this intent I beheld the Shewing with all my diligence: for in all this blessed Shewing I beheld it as one in God's meaning.

All this was shewed by three [ways]: that is to say, by bodily sight, and by word formed in mine understanding, and by spiritual sight. But the spiritual sight I cannot nor may not shew it as openly nor as fully as I would. But I trust in our Lord God Almighty that He shall of His goodness, and for your love, make you to take it more spiritually and more sweetly than I can or may tell it.

THE SECOND REVELATION

CHAPTER X

"God willeth to be seen and to be sought: to be abided and to be trusted"

And after this I saw with bodily sight in the face of the crucifix that hung before me, on the which I gazed continually, a part of His Passion: despite, spitting and sullying, and buffetting, and many languoring pains, more than I can tell, and often changing of colour. And one time I saw half the face, beginning at the ear, over-gone with dry blood till it covered to the mid-face. And after that the other half [was] covered on the same wise, the whiles in this [first] part [it vanished] even as it came.

This saw I bodily, troublously and darkly; and I desired more bodily sight, to have seen more clearly. And I was answered in my reason: *If God will shew thee more, He shall be thy light: thee needeth none but Him.* For I saw Him sought.

For we are now so blind and unwise that we never seek God till He of His goodness shew Himself to us. And when we aught see of Him graciously, then are we stirred by the same grace to seek with great desire to see Him more blissfully.

And thus I saw Him, and sought Him; and I had Him, I wanted Him. And this is, and should be, our common working in this [life], as to my sight.

One time mine understanding was led down into the sea-ground, and there I saw hills and dales green, seeming as it were moss-be-grown, with wrack and gravel. Then I understood thus: that if a man or woman were under the broad water, if he might have sight of God so as God is with a man continually, he should be safe in body and soul, and take no harm: and overpassing, he should have more solace and comfort than all this world can tell. For He willeth we should believe that we see Him continually though that to us it seemeth but little [of sight]; and in this belief He maketh us evermore to gain grace. For He will be seen and He will be sought: He will be abided and he will be trusted.

This Second Shewing was so low and so little and so simple, that my spirits were in great travail in the beholding,—mourning, full of dread, and longing: for I was some time in doubt whether it was a Shewing. And then diverse times our good Lord gave me more sight, whereby I understood truly that it was a Shewing. It was a figure and likeness of our foul deeds' shame that our fair, bright, blessed Lord bare for our sins: it made me to think of the Holy Vernacle at Rome, which He hath portrayed with His own blessed face when He was in His hard Passion, with steadfast will going to His death, and often changing of colour. Of the brownness and blackness, the ruefulness and wastedness of this Image many marvel how it might be, since that He portrayed it with His blessed Face who is the fairness of heaven, flower of earth, and the fruit of the Maiden's womb. Then how might this Image be so darkening in colour and so far from fair?—I desire to tell like as I have understood by the grace of God:—

We know in our Faith, and believe by the teaching and preaching of Holy Church, that the blessed Trinity made Mankind to His image and to His likeness. In the same manner-wise we know that when man fell so deep and so wretchedly by sin, there was none other help to restore man but through Him that made man. And He that made man for love, by the same love He would restore man to the same bliss, and overpassing; and like as we were like-made to the Trinity in our first making, our Maker would that we should be like Jesus Christ, Our Saviour, in heaven without end, by the virtue of our again-making.

Then atwix these two, He would for love and worship of man make Himself as like to man in this deadly life, in our foulness and our wretchedness, as man might be without guilt. This is that which is meant where it is said afore: it was the image and likeness of our foul black deeds' shame wherein our fair, bright, blessed Lord God was hid. But full certainly I dare say, and we ought to trow it, that so fair a man was never none but He, till what time His fair colour was changed with travail and sorrow and Passion and dying. Of this it is spoken in the Eighth Revelation, where it treateth more of the same likeness. And where it speaketh of the Vernacle of Rome, it meaneth by [reason of] diverse changing of colour and countenance, sometime more comfortably and life-like, sometime more ruefully and death-like, as it may be seen in the Eighth Revelation.

And this [dim] vision was a learning, to mine understanding, that the continual seeking of the soul pleaseth God full greatly: for it may do no more than seek, suffer and trust. And this is wrought in the soul that hath it, by the Holy Ghost; and the clearness of finding, *it* is of His special grace, when it is His will. The seeking, with faith, hope, and charity, pleaseth our Lord, and the finding pleaseth the soul and fulfilleth it with joy. And thus was I learned, to mine understanding, that seeking is as good as beholding, for the time that He will suffer the soul to be in travail. It is God's will that *we seek Him*, to the beholding of Him, for by *that* He shall shew us Himself of His special grace when He will. And how a soul shall have Him in its beholding, He shall teach Himself: and that is most worship to Him and profit to thyself, and [the soul thus] most receiveth of meekness and virtues with the grace and leading of the Holy Ghost. For a soul that only fasteneth it[self] on to God with very trust, either by seeking or in beholding, it is the most worship that it may do to Him, as to my sight.

These are two workings that may be seen in this Vision: the one is seeking, the other is beholding. The seeking is common,—that every soul may have with His grace,—and ought to have that discretion and teaching of the Holy Church. It is God's will that we have three things in our seeking:—The first is that we seek earnestly and diligently, without sloth, and, as it may be through His grace, without unreasonable heaviness and vain sorrow. The second is, that we abide Him steadfastly for His love, without murmuring and striving against Him, to our life's end: for it shall last but awhile. The third is that we trust in Him mightily of full assured faith. For it is His will that we know that He shall appear suddenly and blissfully to all that love Him.

For His working is privy, and He willeth to be perceived; and His appearing shall be swiftly sudden; and He willeth to be trusted. For He is full gracious and homely: Blessed may He be!

THE THIRD REVELATION

CHAPTER XI

"All thing that is done, it is well done: for our Lord God doeth all."
"Sin is no deed"

And after this I saw God in a Point, that is to say, in mine understanding,—by which sight I saw that He is in all things.

I beheld and considered, seeing and knowing in sight, with a soft dread, and thought: *What is sin?*

For I saw truly that God doeth all-thing, be it never so little. And I saw truly that nothing is done by hap nor by adventure, but all things by the foreseeing wisdom of God: if it be hap or adventure in the sight of man, our blindness and our unforesight is the cause. For the things that are in the foreseeing wisdom of God from without beginning, (which rightfully and worshipfully and continually He leadeth to the best end,) as they come about fall to us suddenly, ourselves unwitting; and thus by our blindness and our unforesight we say: these be haps and adventures. But to our Lord God they be not so.

Wherefore me behoveth needs to grant that all-thing that is done, it is well-done: for our Lord God doeth all. For in this time the working of creatures was not shewed, but [the working] of our Lord God in the creature: for He is in the Mid-point of all thing, and all He doeth. And I was certain He doeth no sin.

And here I saw verily that sin is no deed: for in all this was not sin shewed. And I would no longer marvel in this, but beheld our Lord, what He would shew.

And thus, as much as it might be for the time, the rightfulness of God's working was shewed to the soul.

Rightfulness hath two fair properties: it is right and it is full. And so are all the works of our Lord God: thereto needeth neither the working of mercy nor grace: for they be all rightful: wherein faileth nought.

But in another time He gave a Shewing for the beholding of sin nakedly, as I shall tell: where He useth working of mercy and grace.

And this vision was shewed, to mine understanding, for that our Lord would have the soul turned truly unto the beholding of Him, and generally of all His works. For they are full good; and all His doings are easy and sweet, and to great ease bringing the soul that is turned from the beholding of the blind Deeming of man unto the fair sweet Deeming of our Lord God. For a man beholdeth some deeds well done and some deeds evil, but our Lord beholdeth them not so: for as all that hath being in nature is of Godly making, so is all that is done, in property of God's doing. For it is easy to understand that the best deed is well done: and so well as the best deed is done—the highest— so well is the least deed done; and all thing in its property and in the order that our Lord hath ordained it to from without beginning. For there is no doer but He.

I saw full surely that he changeth never His purpose in no manner of thing, nor never shall, without end. For there was no thing unknown to Him in His rightful ordinance from without beginning. And therefore all-thing was set in order ere anything was made, as it should stand without end; and no manner of thing shall fail of that point. For He made all things in fulness of goodness, and therefore the blessed Trinity is ever full pleased in all His works.

And all this shewed He full blissfully, signifying thus: *See! I am God: see! I am in all thing: see! I do all thing: see! I lift never mine hands off my works, nor ever shall, without end: see! I lead all thing to the end I ordained it to from without beginning, by the same Might, Wisdom and Love whereby I made it. How should any thing be amiss?*

Thus mightily, wisely, and lovingly was the soul examined in this Vision. Then saw I soothly that me behoved, of need, to assent, with great reverence enjoying in God.

THE FOURTH REVELATION

CHAPTER XII

"The dearworthy blood of our Lord Jesus Christ as verily as it is most precious, so verily it it most plenteous"

And after this I saw, beholding, the body plenteously bleeding in seeming of the Scourging, as thus:—The fair skin was broken full deep into the tender flesh with sharp smiting all about the sweet body. So plenteously the hot blood ran out that there was neither seen skin nor wound, but as it were all blood. And when it came where it should have fallen down, then it vanished. Notwithstanding, the bleeding continued awhile: till it might be seen and considered. And this was so plenteous, to my sight, that methought if it had been so in kind and in substance at that time, it should have made the bed all one blood, and have passed over about.

And then came to my mind that God hath made waters plenteous in earth to our service and to our bodily ease for tender love that He hath to us, but yet liketh Him better that we take full homely His blessed blood to wash us of sin: for there is no water that is made that He liketh so well to give us. For it is most plenteous as it is most precious: and that by the virtue of His blessed Godhead; and it is [of] our Kind, and all-blissfully belongeth to us by the virtue of His precious love.

The dearworthy blood of our Lord Jesus Christ as verily as it is most precious, so verily it is most plenteous. Behold and see! The precious plenty of His dearworthy blood descended down into Hell and burst her bands and delivered all that were there which belonged to the Court of Heaven. The precious plenty of His dearworthy blood overfloweth all Earth, and is ready to wash all creatures of sin, which be of goodwill, have been, and shall be. The precious plenty of His dearworthy blood ascended up into Heaven to the blessed body of our Lord Jesus Christ, and there is in Him, bleeding and praying for us to the Father,—and is, and shall be as long as it needeth;—and ever shall be as long as it needeth. And evermore it floweth in all Heavens enjoying the salvation of all mankind, that are there, and shall be—fulfilling the number that faileth.

THE FIFTH REVELATION

CHAPTER XIII

"The Enemy is overcome by the blessed Passion and Death of our
Lord Jesus Christ"

And after this, ere God shewed any words, He suffered me for a
convenient time to give heed unto Him and all that I had seen, and all
intellect that was therein, as the simplicity of the soul might take it.
Then He, without voice and opening of lips, formed in my soul these
words: *Herewith is the Fiend overcome.* These words said our Lord,
meaning His blessed Passion as He shewed it afore.

On this shewed our Lord that the Passion of Him is the overcoming
of the Fiend. God shewed that the Fiend hath now the same malice
that he had afore the Incarnation. And as sore he travaileth, and as
continually he seeth that all souls of salvation escape him,
worshipfully, by the virtue of Christ's precious Passion. And that is his
sorrow, and full evil is he ashamed: for all that God suffereth him to
do turneth [for] us to joy and [for] him to shame and woe. And he hath
as much sorrow when God giveth him leave to work, as when he
worketh not: and that is for that he may never do as ill as he would:
for his might is all taken into God's hand.

But in God there may be no wrath, as to my sight: for our good Lord
endlessly hath regard to His own worship and to the profit of all that
shall be saved. With might and right He withstandeth the Reproved,
the which of malice and wickedness busy them to contrive and to do
against God's will. Also I saw our Lord scorn his malice and set at
nought his unmight; and He willeth that we do so. For this sight I
laughed mightily, and that made them to laugh that were about me,
and their laughing was a pleasure to me. I thought that I would that all
mine even-Christians had seen as I saw, and then would they all laugh
with me. But I saw not Christ laugh. For I understood that we may
laugh in comforting of ourselves and joying in God for that the devil
is overcome. And when I saw Him scorn his malice, it was by leading
of mine understanding into our Lord: that is to say, it was an inward
shewing of verity, without changing of look. For, as to my sight, it is a
worshipful property of God's that [He] is ever the same.

And after this I fell into a graveness, and said: *I see three things: I see game, scorn, and earnest. I see [a] game, in that the Fiend is overcome; I see scorn, in that God scorneth him, and he shall be scorned; and I see earnest, in that he is overcome by the blissful Passion and Death of our Lord Jesus Christ that was done in full earnest and with sober travail.*

When I said, *he is scorned,*—I meant that God scorneth him, that is to say, because He seeth him now as he shall do without end. For in this [word] God shewed that the Fiend is condemned. And this meant I when I said: *he shall be scorned*: [he shall be scorned] at Doomsday, generally of all that shall be saved, to whose consolation he hath great ill-will. For then he shall see that all the woe and tribulation that he hath done to them shall be turned to increase of their joy, without end; and all the pain and tribulation that he would have brought them to shall endlessly go with him to hell.

THE SIXTH REVELATION

CHAPTER XIV

"The age of every man shall be acknowledged before him in Heaven, and every man shall be rewarded for his willing service and for his time"

After this our good Lord said: *I thank thee for thy travail, and especially for thy youth.*

And in this [Shewing] mine understanding was lifted up into Heaven where I saw our Lord as a lord in his own house, which hath called all his dear worthy servants and friends to a stately feast. Then I saw the Lord take no place in His own house, but I saw Him royally reign in His house, fulfilling it with joy and mirth, Himself endlessly to gladden and to solace His dearworthy friends, full homely and full courteously, with marvellous melody of endless love, in His own fair blessed Countenance. Which glorious Countenance of the Godhead fulfilleth the Heavens with joy and bliss.

God shewed three degrees of bliss that every soul shall have in Heaven that willingly hath served God in any degree in earth. The first is the worshipful thanks of our Lord God that he shall receive when he is delivered of pain. This thanking is so high and so worshipful that the soul thinketh it filleth him though there were no more. For methought that all the pain and travail that might be suffered by all living men might not deserve the worshipful thanks that one man shall have that willingly hath served God. The second is that all the blessed creatures that are in Heaven shall see that worshipful thanking, and He maketh his service known to all that are in Heaven. And here this example was shewed:—A king, if he thank his servants, it is a great worship to them, and if he maketh it known to all the realm, then is the worship greatly increased.—The third is, that as new and as gladdening as it is received in that time, right so shall it last without end.

And I saw that homely and sweetly was this shewed, and that the age of every man shall be [made] known in Heaven, and [he] shall be rewarded for his willing service and for his time. And specially the age of them that willingly and freely offer their youth unto God, passingly is rewarded and wonderfully is thanked.

For I saw that whene'er what time a man or woman is truly turned to God,—for one day's service and for his endless will he shall have all these three decrees of bliss. And the more the loving soul seeth this courtesy of God, the liefer he is to serve him all the days of his life.

THE SEVENTH REVELATION

CHAPTER XV

"It is not God's will that we follow the feeling of pains in sorrow and mourning for them"

And after this He shewed a sovereign ghostly pleasante in my soul. I was fulfilled with the everlasting sureness, mightily sustained without any painful dread. This feeling was so glad and so ghostly that I was in all peace and in rest, that there was nothing in earth that should have grieved me.

This lasted but a while, and I was turned and left to myself in heaviness, and weariness of my life, and irksomeness of myself, that scarcely I could have patience to live. There was no comfort nor none ease to me but faith, hope, and charity; and these I had in truth, but little in feeling.

And anon after this our blessed Lord gave me again the comfort and the rest in soul, in satisfying and sureness so blissful and so mighty that no dread, no sorrow, no pain bodily that might be suffered should have distressed me. And then the pain shewed again to my feeling, and then the joy and the pleasing, and now that one, and now that other, divers times—I suppose about twenty times. And in the time of joy I might have said with Saint Paul: *Nothing shall dispart me from the charity of Christ*; and in the pain I might have said with Peter: *Lord, save me: I perish!*

This Vision was shewed me, according to mine understanding, [for] that it is speedful to some souls to feel on this wise: sometime to be in comfort, and sometime to fail and to be left to themselves. God willeth that we know that He keepeth us even alike secure in woe and in weal. And for profit of man's soul, a man is sometime left to himself; although sin is not always the cause: for in this time I sinned not wherefore I should be left to myself—for it was so sudden. Also I deserved not to have this blessed feeling. But freely our Lord giveth when He will; and suffereth us [to be] in woe sometime. And both is one love.

For it is God's will that we hold us in comfort with all our might: for bliss is lasting without end, and pain is passing and shall be brought to nought for them that shall be saved. And therefore it is not God's will that we follow the feelings of pain in sorrow and mourning for them, but that we suddenly pass over, and hold us in endless enjoyment.

THE EIGHTH REVELATION

CHAPTER XVI

"A Part of His Passion"

After this Christ shewed a part of His Passion near His dying.

I saw His sweet face as it were dry and bloodless with pale dying. And later, more pale, dead, languoring; and then turned more dead unto blue; and then more brown-blue, as the flesh turned more deeply dead. For His Passion shewed to me most specially in His blessed face (and chiefly in His lips): there I saw these four colours, though it were afore fresh, ruddy, and pleasing, to my sight. This was a pitiful change to see, this deep dying. And also the [inward] moisture clotted and dried, to my sight, and the sweet body was brown and black, all turned out of fair, life-like colour of itself, unto dry dying.

For that same time that our Lord and blessed Saviour died upon the Rood, it was a dry, hard wind, and wondrous cold, as to my sight, and what time [all] the precious blood was bled out of the sweet body that might pass therefrom, yet there dwelled a moisture in the sweet flesh of Christ, as it was shewed.

Bloodlessness and pain dried within; and blowing of wind and cold coming from without met together in the sweet body of Christ. And these four,—twain without, and twain within—dried the flesh of Christ by process of time. And though this pain was bitter and sharp, it was full long lasting, as to my sight, and painfully dried up all the lively spirits of Christ's flesh. Thus I saw the sweet flesh dry in seeming by part after part, with marvellous pains. And as long as any spirit had life in Christ's flesh, so long suffered He pain.

This long pining seemed to me as if He had been seven nights dead, dying, at the point of outpassing away, suffering the last pain. And when I said it seemed to me as if He had been seven night dead, it meaneth that the sweet body was so discoloured, so dry, so shrunken, so deathly, and so piteous, as if He had been seven night dead, continually dying. And methought the drying of Christ's flesh was the most pain, and the last, of His Passion.

CHAPTER XVII

"How might any pain be more to me than to see Him that is all my life, and all my bliss, and all my joy suffer?"

And in this dying was brought to my mind the words of Christ: *I thirst.*

For I saw in Christ a double thirst: one bodily; another spiritual, the which I shall speak of in the Thirty-first Chapter.

For this word was shewed for the bodily thirst: the which I understood was caused by failing of moisture. For the blessed flesh and bones was left all alone without blood and moisture. The blessed body dried alone long time with wringing of the nails and weight of the body. For I understood that for tenderness of the sweet hands and of the sweet feet, by the greatness, hardness, and grievousness of the nails the wounds waxed wide and the body sagged, for weight by long time hanging. And [therewith was] piercing and pressing of the head, and binding of the Crown all baked with dry blood, with the sweet hair clinging, and the dry flesh, to the thorns, and the thorns to the flesh drying; and in the beginning while the flesh was fresh and bleeding, the continual sitting of the thorns made the wounds wide. And furthermore I saw that the sweet skin and the tender flesh, with the hair and the blood, was all raised and loosed about from the bone, with the thorns where-through it were rent in many pieces, as a cloth that were sagging, as if it would hastily have fallen off, for heaviness and looseness, while it had natural moisture. And that was great sorrow and dread to me: for methought I would not for my life have seen it fall. How it was done I saw not; but understood it was with the sharp thorns and the violent and grievous setting on of the Garland of Thorns, unsparingly and without pity. This continued awhile, and soon it began to change, and I beheld and marvelled how it might be. And then I saw it was because it began to dry, and stint a part of the weight, and set about the Garland. And thus it encircled all about, as it were garland upon garland. The Garland of the Thorns was dyed with the blood, and that other garland [of Blood] and the head, all was one colour, as clotted blood when it is dry. The skin of the flesh that shewed (of the face and of the body), was small-rimpled with a tanned colour, like a dry board when it is aged; and the face more brown than the body.

I saw four manner of dryings: the first was bloodlessness; the second was pain following after; the third, hanging up in the air, as men hang a cloth to dry; the fourth, that the bodily Kind asked liquid and there was no manner of comfort ministered to Him in all His woe and distress. Ah! hard and grievous was his pain, but much more hard and grievous it was when the moisture failed and began to dry thus, shrivelling.

These were the pains that shewed in the blessed head: the first wrought to the dying, while it had moisture; and that other, slow, with shrinking drying, [and] with blowing of the wind from without, that dried and pained Him with cold more than mine heart can think.

And other pains—for which pains I saw that all is too little that I can say: for it may not be told.

The which Shewing of Christ's pains filled me full of pain. For I wist well He suffered but once, but [this was as if] He would shew it me and fill me with mind as I had afore desired. And in all this time of Christ's pains I felt no pain but for Christ's pains. Then thought-me: *I knew but little what pain it was that I asked*; and, as a wretch, repented me, thinking: *If I had wist what it had been, loth me had been to have prayed it.* For methought it passed bodily death, my pains.

I thought: *Is any pain like this?* And I was answered in my reason: *Hell is another pain: for there is despair. But of all pains that lead to salvation this is the most pain, to see thy Love suffer. How might any pain be more to me than to see Him that is all my life, all my bliss, and all my joy, suffer?* Here felt I soothfastly that I loved Christ so much above myself that there was no pain that might be suffered like to that sorrow that I had to [see] Him in pain.

CHAPTER XVIII

"When He was in pain, we were in pain"

Here I saw a part of the compassion of our Lady, Saint Mary: for Christ and she were so oned in love that the greatness of her loving was cause of the greatness of her pain. For in this [Shewing] I saw a Substance of Nature's Love, continued by Grace, that creatures have to Him: which Kind Love was most fully shewed in His sweet Mother, and overpassing; for so much as she loved Him more than all other, her pains passed all other. For ever the higher, the mightier, the sweeter that the love be, the more sorrow it is to the lover to see that body in pain that is loved.

And all His disciples and all His true lovers suffered pains more than their own bodily dying. For I am sure by mine own feeling that the least of them loved Him so far above himself that it passeth all that I can say.

Here saw I a great oneing betwixt Christ and us, to mine understanding: for when He was in pain, we were in pain.

And all creatures that ought suffer pain, suffered with Him: that is to say, all creatures that God hath made to our service. The firmament, the earth, failed for sorrow in their Nature in the time of Christ's dying. For it belongeth naturally to their property to know Him for their God, in whom all their virtue standeth: when He failed, then behoved it needs to them, because of kindness [between them], to fail with Him, as much as they might, for sorrow of His pains.

And thus they that were His friends suffered pain for love. And, generally, *all*: that is to say, they that knew Him not suffered for failing of all manner of comfort save the mighty, privy keeping of God. I speak of two manner of folk, as they may be understood by two persons: the one was Pilate, the other was Saint Dionyse of France, which was [at] that time a Paynim. For when he saw wondrous and marvellous sorrows and dreads that befell in that time, he said: *Either the world is now at an end, or He that is Maker of Kind suffereth.* Wherefore he did write on an altar: This is the Altar of Unknown God. God that of His goodness maketh the planets and the elements to work of Kind to the blessed man and the cursed, in that time made withdrawing of it from both; wherefore it was that they that knew Him not were in sorrow that time.

Thus was our Lord Jesus made-naught for us; and all we stand in this manner made-naught with Him, and shall do till we come to His bliss; as I shall tell after.

CHAPTER XIX

"Thus was I learned to choose Jesus for my Heaven, whom I saw only in pain at that time"

In this [time] I would have looked up from the Cross, but I durst not. For I wist well that while I beheld in the Cross I was surely-safe; therefore I would not assent to put my soul in peril: for away from the Cross was no sureness, for frighting of fiends.

Then had I a proffer in my reason, as if it had been friendly said to me: *Look up to Heaven to His Father.* And then saw I well, with the faith that I felt, that there was nothing betwixt the Cross and Heaven that might have harmed me. Either me behoved to look up or else to answer. I answered inwardly with all the might of my soul, and said: *Nay; I may not: for Thou art my Heaven.* This I said for that I would not. For I would liever have been in that pain till Doomsday than to come to Heaven otherwise than by Him. For I wist well that He that bound me so sore, He should unbind me when that He would. Thus was I learned to choose Jesus to my Heaven, whom I saw only in pain at that time: meliked no other Heaven than Jesus, which shall be my bliss when I come there.

And this hath ever been a comfort to me, that I chose Jesus to my Heaven, by His grace, in all this time of Passion and sorrow; and that hath been a learning to me that I should evermore do so: choose only Jesus to my Heaven in weal and woe.

And though I as a wretched creature had repented me (I said afore if I had wist what pain it would be, I had been loth to have prayed), here saw I truly that it was reluctance and frailty of the flesh without assent of the soul: to which God assigneth no blame. Repenting and willing choice be two contraries which I felt both in one at that time. And these be [of our] two parts: the one outward, the other inward. The outward part is our deadly flesh-hood, which is now in pain and woe, and shall be, in this life: whereof I felt much in this time; and that part it was that repented. The inward part is an high, blissful life, which is all in peace and in love: and this was more inwardly felt; and this part is [that] in which mightily, wisely and with steadfast will I chose Jesus to my Heaven.

And in this I saw verily that the inward part is master and sovereign to the outward, and doth not charge itself with, nor take heed to, the will of that: but all the intent and will is set to be oned unto our Lord Jesus. That the outward part should draw the inward to assent was not shewed to me; but that the inward draweth the outward by grace, and both shall be oned in bliss without end, by the virtue of Christ,—*this* was shewed.

CHAPTER XX

"For every man's sin that shall be saved He suffered, and every man's sorrow and desolation He saw, and sorrowed for Kinship and Love"

And thus I saw our Lord Jesus languoring long time. For the oneing with the Godhead gave strength to the manhood for love to suffer more than all men might suffer: I mean not only more pain than all men might suffer, but also that He suffered more pain than all men of salvation that ever were from the first beginning unto the last day might tell or fully think, having regard to the worthiness of the highest worshipful King and the shameful, despised, painful death. For He that is highest and worthiest was most fully made-nought and most utterly despised.

For the highest point that may be seen in the Passion is to think and know what He is that suffered. And in this [Shewing] He brought in part to mind the height and nobleness of the glorious Godhead, and therewith the preciousness and the tenderness of the blessed Body, which be together united; and also the lothness that is in our Kind to suffer pain. For as much as He was most tender and pure, right so He was most strong and mighty to suffer.

And for every man's sin that shall be saved He suffered: and every man's sorrow and desolation He saw, and sorrowed for Blindness and love. (For in as much as our Lady sorrowed for His pains, in so much He suffered sorrow for her sorrow;—and more, in as greatly as the sweet manhood of Him was worthier in Kind.) For as long as He was passible He suffered for us and sorrowed *for* us; and now He is uprisen and no more passible, yet He suffereth *with* us.

And I, beholding all this by His grace, saw that the Love of Him was so strong which He hath to our soul that willingly He chose it with great desire, and mildly He suffered it with well-pleasing.

For the soul that beholdeth it thus, when it is touched by grace, it shall verily see that the pains of Christ's Passion pass all pains: [all pains] that is to say, which shall be turned into everlasting, o'erpassing joys by the virtue of Christ's Passion.

CHAPTER XXI

"We be now with Him in His Pains and His Passion, dying. We shall be with Him in Heaven. Through learning in this little pain that we suffer here, we shall have an high endless knowledge of God which we could never have without that"

It is God's will, as to mine understanding, that we have Three Manners of Beholding His blessed Passion. The First is: *the hard Pain that He suffered*,—[beholding it] with contrition and compassion. And that shewed our Lord in this time, and gave me strength and grace to see it.

And I looked for the departing with all my might, and thought to have seen the body all dead; but I saw Him not so. And right in the same time that methought, by the seeming, the life might no longer last and the Shewing of the end behoved needs to be,—suddenly (I beholding in the same Cross), He changed [the look of] His blessed Countenance. The changing of His blessed Countenance changed mine, and I was as glad and merry as it was possible. Then brought our Lord merrily to my mind: *Where is now any point of the pain, or of thy grief?* And I was full merry.

I understood that we be now, in our Lord's meaning, in His Cross with Him in His pains and His Passion, dying; and we, willingly abiding in the same Cross with His help and His grace unto the last point, suddenly He shall change His Cheer to us, and we shall be with Him in Heaven. Betwixt that one and that other shall be no time, and then shall all be brought to joy. And thus said He in this Shewing: *Where is now any point of thy pain, or thy grief?* And we shall be full blessed.

And here saw I verily that if He shewed now [to] us His *Blissful* Cheer, there is no pain in earth or in other place that should aggrieve us; but all things should be to us joy and bliss. But because He sheweth to us time of His Passion, as He bare it in *this* life, and His Cross, therefore we are in distress and travail, with Him, as our frailty asketh. And the cause why He suffereth [it to be so,] is for [that] He will of His goodness make us the higher with Him in His bliss; and for this little pain that we suffer here, we shall have an high endless knowing in God which we could never have without that. And the harder our pains have been with Him in His Cross, the more shall our worship be with Him in His Kingdom.

THE NINTH REVELATION

CHAPTER XXII

"The Love that made Him to suffer passeth so far all His Pains as
Heaven is above Earth"

Then said our good Lord Jesus Christ: *Art thou well pleased that I
suffered for thee?* I said: *Yea, good Lord, I thank Thee; Yea, good Lord,
blessed mayst Thou be.* Then said Jesus, our kind Lord: *If thou art
pleased, I am pleased: it is a joy, a bliss, an endless satisfying to me
that ever suffered I Passion for thee; and if I might suffer more, I would
suffer more.*

In this feeling my understanding was lifted up into Heaven, and there
I saw three heavens: of which sight I marvelled greatly. And though I
see three heavens—and all in the blessed manhood of Christ—none
is more, none is less, none is higher, none is lower, but [they are] even-
like in bliss.

For the First Heaven, Christ shewed me His Father; in no bodily
likeness, but in His property and in His working. That is to say, I saw
in Christ that the Father is. The working of the Father is this, that He
giveth meed to His Son Jesus Christ. This gift and this meed is so
blissful to Jesus that His Father might have given Him no meed that
might have pleased Him better. The first heaven, that is the pleasing
of the Father, shewed to me as one heaven; and it was full blissful: for
He is full pleased with all the deeds that Jesus hath done about our
salvation. Wherefore we be not only His by His buying, but also by
the courteous gift of His Father we be His bliss, we be His meed, we
be His worship, we be His crown. (And this was a singular marvel and
a full delectable beholding, that we be His crown!) This that I say is so
great bliss to Jesus that He setteth at nought all His travail, and His
hard Passion, and His cruel and shameful death.

And in these words: *If that I might suffer more, I would suffer more,—*
I saw in truth that as often as He *might* die, so often He *would,* and
love should never let Him have rest till He had done it. And I beheld
with great diligence for to learn how often He would die if He might.
And verily the number passed mine understanding and my wits so far
that my reason might not, nor could, comprehend it. And when He

had thus oft died, or should, yet He would set it at nought, for love: for all seemeth Him but little in regard of His love.

For though the sweet manhood of Christ might suffer but once, the goodness in Him may never cease of proffer: every day He is ready to the same, if it might be. For if He said He would for my love make new Heavens and new Earth, it were but little in comparison; for this might be done every day if He would, without any travail. But to die for my love so often that the number passeth creature's reason, it is the highest proffer that our Lord God might make to man's soul, as to my sight. Then meaneth He thus: *How should it not be that I should not do for thy love all that I might of deeds which grieve me not, sith I would, for thy love, die so often, having no regard to my hard pains?*

And here saw I, for the Second Beholding in this blessed Passion *the love that made Him to suffer passeth as far all His pains as Heaven is above Earth.* For the pains was a noble, worshipful deed done in a time by the working of love: but Love was without beginning, is, and shall be without ending. For which love He said full sweetly these words: *If I might suffer more, I would suffer more.* He said not, *If it were needful to suffer more:* for though it were not needful, if He *might* suffer more, He would.

This deed, and this work about our salvation, was ordained as well as God might ordain it. And here I saw a Full Bliss in Christ: for His bliss should not have been full, if it might any better have been done.

CHAPTER XXIII

"The Glad Giver"
"All the Trinity wrought in the Passion of Jesus Christ"

And in these three words: *It is a joy, a bliss, an endless satisfying to me*, were shewed three heavens, as thus: For the joy, I understood the pleasure of the Father; and for the bliss, the worship of the Son; and for the endless satisfying, the Holy Ghost. The Father is pleased, the Son is worshipped, the Holy Ghost is satisfied.

And here saw I, for the Third Beholding in His blissful Passion: that is to say, *the Joy and the Bliss that make Him to be well-satisfied in it.* For our Courteous Lord shewed His Passion to me in five manners:

of which the first is the bleeding of the head; the second is, discolouring of His face; the third is, the plenteous bleeding of the body, in seeming [as] from the scourging; the fourth is, the deep dying:—these four are aforetold for the pains of the Passion. And the fifth is [this] that was shewed for the joy and the bliss of the Passion.

For it is God's will that we have true enjoying with Him in our salvation, and therein He willeth [that] we be mightily comforted and strengthened; and thus willeth He that merrily with His grace our soul be occupied. For we are His bliss: for in us He enjoyeth without end; and so shall we in Him, with His grace.

And all that He hath done for us, and doeth, and ever shall, was never cost nor charge to Him, nor might be, but only that [which] He did in our manhood, beginning at the sweet Incarnation and lasting to the Blessed Uprise on Easter-morrow: so long dured the cost and the charge about our redemption in *deed*: of [the] which deed He enjoyeth endlessly, as it is aforesaid.

Jesus willeth that we take heed to the bliss that is in the blessed Trinity [because] of our salvation and that *we* desire to have as much spiritual enjoying, with His grace, (as it is aforesaid): that is to say, that the enjoying of our salvation be [as] like to the joy that Christ hath of our salvation as it may be while we are here.

All the Trinity wrought in the Passion of Christ, ministering abundance of virtues and plenty of grace to us by Him: but only the Maiden's Son suffered: whereof all the blessed Trinity endlessly enjoyeth. All this was shewed in these words: *Art thou well pleased?—* and by that other word that Christ said: *If thou art pleased, then am I pleased;—*as if He said: *It is joy and satisfying enough to me, and I ask nought else of thee for my travail but that I might well please thee.*

And in this He brought to mind the property of a glad giver. A glad giver taketh but little heed of the thing that he giveth, but all his desire and all his intent is to please him and solace him to whom he giveth it. And if the receiver take the gift highly and thankfully, then the courteous giver setteth at nought all his cost and all his travail, for joy and delight that he hath pleased and solaced him that he loveth. Plenteously and fully was this shewed.

Think also wisely of the greatness of this word "*ever*." For in it was shewed an high knowing of love that *He* hath in our salvation, with manifold joys that follow of the Passion of Christ. One is that He rejoiceth that He hath done it in deed, and He shall no more suffer; another, that He bought us from endless pains of hell.

THE TENTH REVELATION

CHAPTER XXIV

"Our Lord looked unto His [wounded] Side, and beheld, rejoicing....
Lo! how I loved thee"

Then with a glad cheer our Lord looked unto His Side and beheld, rejoicing. With His sweet looking He led forth the understanding of His creature by the same wound into His Side within. And then he shewed a fair, delectable place, and large enough for all mankind that shall be saved to rest in peace and in love. And therewith He brought to mind His dearworthy blood and precious water which he let pour all out for love. And with the sweet beholding He shewed His blessed heart even cloven in two.

And with this sweet enjoying, He shewed unto mine understanding, in part, *the blessed Godhead*, stirring then the poor soul to understand, as it may be said, that is, to think on, the *endless* Love that was without beginning, and is, and shall be ever. And with this our good Lord said full blissfully: *Lo, how that I loved thee,* as if He had said: *My darling, behold and see thy Lord, thy God that is thy Maker and thine endless joy, see what satisfying and bliss I have in thy salvation; and for my love rejoice [thou] with me.*

And also, for more understanding, this blessed word was said: *Lo, how I loved thee! Behold and see that I loved thee so much ere I died for thee that I would die for thee; and now I have died for thee and suffered willingly that which I may. And now is all my bitter pain and all my hard travail turned to endless joy and bliss to me and to thee. How should it now be that thou shouldst anything pray that pleaseth me but that I should full gladly grant it thee? For my pleasing is thy holiness and thine endless joy and bliss with me.*

This is the understanding, simply as I can say it, of this blessed word: *Lo, how I loved thee.* This shewed our good Lord for to make us glad and merry.

THE ELEVENTH REVELATION

CHAPTER XXV

"I wot well that thou wouldst see my blessed Mother...."
"Wilt thou see in her how thou art loved?"

And with this same cheer of mirth and joy our good Lord looked down on the right side and brought to my mind where our Lady stood in the time of His Passion; and said: *Wilt thou see her?* And in this sweet word [it was] as if He had said: *I wot well that thou wouldst see my blessed Mother: for, after myself, she is the highest joy that I might shew thee, and most pleasance and worship to me; and most she is desired to be seen of my blessed creatures.* And for the high, marvellous, singular love that He hath to this sweet Maiden, His blessed Mother, our Lady Saint Mary, He shewed her highly rejoicing, as by the meaning of these sweet words; as if He said: *Wilt thou see how I love her, that thou mightest joy with me in the love that I have in her and she in me?*

And also (unto more understanding this sweet word) our Lord speaketh to all mankind that shall be saved, as it were all to one person, as if He said: *Wilt thou see in her how thou art loved? For thy love I made her so high, so noble and so worthy; and this pleaseth me, and so will I that it doeth thee.*

For after Himself she is the most blissful sight.

But hereof am I not learned to long to see her bodily presence while I am here, but the virtues of her blessed soul: her truth, her wisdom, her charity; whereby I may learn to know myself and reverently dread my God. And when our good Lord had shewed this and said this word: *Wilt thou see her?* I answered and said: *Yea, good Lord, I thank Thee; yea, good Lord, if it be Thy will.* Oftentimes I prayed this, and I weened to have seen her in bodily presence, but I saw her not so. And Jesus in that word shewed me ghostly sight of her: right as I had seen her afore little and simple, so He shewed her then high and noble and glorious, and pleasing to Him above all creatures.

And He willeth that it be known; that [so] all those that please them in Him should please them in her, and in the pleasance that He hath in her and she in Him. And, to more understanding, He shewed this example: *As if a man love a creature singularly, above all creatures,* he willeth to make all creatures to love and to have pleasance in that creature that he loveth so greatly. And in this word that Jesus said: *Wilt thou see her?* methought it was the most pleasing word that He might have given me of her, with that ghostly Shewing that He gave me of her. For our Lord shewed me nothing in special but our Lady Saint Mary; and her He shewed three times. The first was as she was with Child; the second was as she was in her sorrows under the Cross; the third is as she is now in pleasing, worship, and joy.

THE TWELFTH REVELATION

CHAPTER XXVI

"It is I, it is I"

And after this our Lord shewed Himself more glorified, as to my sight, than I saw Him before [in the Shewing] wherein I was learned that our soul shall never have rest till it cometh to Him, knowing that He is fulness of joy, homely and courteous, blissful and very life.

Our Lord Jesus oftentimes said: *I it am, I it am: I it am that is highest, I it am that thou lovest, I it am that thou enjoyest, I it am that thou servest, I it am that thou longest for, I it am that thou desirest, I it am that thou meanest, I it am that is all. I it am that Holy Church preacheth and teacheth thee, I it am that shewed me here to thee.* The number of the words passeth my wit and all my understanding and all my powers. And they are the highest, as to my sight: for therein is comprehended—I cannot tell,—but the joy that I saw in the Shewing of them passeth all that heart may wish for and soul may desire. Therefore the words be not declared here; but every man after the grace that God giveth him in understanding and loving, receive them in our Lord's meaning.

THE THIRTEENTH REVELATION

CHAPTER XXVII

Often I wondered why by the great foreseeing wisdom of God the beginning of sin was not hindered: for then, methought, all should have been well." "Sin is behovable—[playeth a needful part]—; but all shall be well"

After this the Lord brought to my mind the longing that I had to Him afore. And I saw that nothing letted me but sin. And so I looked, generally, upon us all, and methought: *If sin had not been, we should all have been clean and like to our Lord, as He made us.*

And thus, in my folly, afore this time often I wondered why by the great foreseeing wisdom of God the beginning of sin was not letted: for then, methought, all should have been well. This stirring [of mind] was much to be forsaken, but nevertheless mourning and sorrow I made therefor, without reason and discretion.

But Jesus, who in this Vision informed me of all that is needful to me, answered by this word and said: *It behoved that there should be sin; but all shall be well, and all shall be well, and all manner of thing shall be well.*

In this naked word *sin*, our Lord brought to my mind, generally, *all that is not good*, and the shameful despite and the utter noughting that He bare for us in this life, and His dying; and all the pains and passions of all His creatures, ghostly and bodily; (for we be all partly noughted, and we shall be noughted following our Master, Jesus, till we be full purged, that is to say, till we be fully noughted of our deadly flesh and of all our inward affections which are not very good;) and the beholding of this, with all pains that ever were or ever shall be,—and with all these I understand the Passion of Christ for most pain, and overpassing. All this was shewed in a touch and quickly passed over into comfort: for our good Lord would not that the soul were affeared of this terrible sight.

But I saw not *sin*: for I believe it hath no manner of substance nor no part of being, nor could it be known but by the pain it is cause of.

And thus pain, *it* is something, as to my sight, for a time; for it purgeth, and maketh us to know ourselves and to ask mercy. For the Passion of our Lord is comfort to us against all this, and so is His blessed will. And for the tender love that our good Lord hath to all that shall be saved, He comforteth readily and sweetly, signifying thus: *It is sooth that sin is cause of all this pain; but all shall be well, and all shall be well, and all manner [of] thing shall be well.*

These words were said full tenderly, showing no manner of blame to me nor to any that shall be saved. Then were it a great unkindness to blame or wonder on God for my sin, since He blameth not me for sin.

And in these words I saw a marvellous high mystery hid in God, which mystery He shall openly make known to us in Heaven: in which knowing we shall verily see the cause why He suffered sin to come. In which sight we shall endlessly joy in our Lord God.

CHAPTER XXVIII

"Each brotherly compassion that man hath on his fellow Christians, with charity, it is Christ in him"

Thus I saw how Christ hath compassion on us for the cause of sin. And right as I was afore in the [Shewing of the] Passion of Christ fulfilled with pain and compassion, like so in this [sight] I was fulfilled, in part, with compassion of all mine even-Christians—for that well, well beloved people that shall be saved. For God's servants, Holy Church, shall be shaken in sorrow and anguish, tribulation in this world, as men shake a cloth in the wind.

And as to this our Lord answered in this manner: *A great thing shall I make hereof in Heaven of endless worship and everlasting joys.*

Yea, so far forth I saw, that our Lord joyeth of the tribulations of His servants, with ruth and compassion. On each person that He loveth, to His bliss for to bring [them], He layeth something that is no blame in His sight, whereby they are blamed and despised in this world, scorned, mocked, and outcasted. And this He doeth for to hinder the harm that they should take from the pomp and the vain-glory of this wretched life, and make their way ready to come to Heaven, and up-raise them in His bliss everlasting. For He saith: *I shall wholly break you of your vain affections and your vicious pride; and after that I shall together gather you, and make you mild and meek, clean and holy, by oneing to me.*

And then I saw that each kind compassion that man hath on his even-Christians with charity, it is Christ in him.

That same noughting that was shewed in His Passion, it was shewed again here in this Compassion. Wherein were two manner of understandings in our Lord's meaning. The one was the bliss that we are brought to, wherein He willeth that we rejoice. The other is for comfort in our pain: for He willeth that we perceive that it shall all be turned to worship and profit by virtue of His passion, that we perceive that we suffer not alone but with Him, and see Him to be our Ground, and that we see His pains and His noughting passeth so far all that we may suffer, that it may not be fully thought.

The beholding of this will save us from murmuring and despair in the feeling of our pains. And if we see soothly that our sin deserveth it, yet His love excuseth us, and of His great courtesy He doeth away all our blame, and beholdeth us with ruth and pity as children innocent and unloathful.

CHAPTER XXIX

"How could all be well, for the great harm that is come by sin to the creature?"

But in this I stood beholding things general, troublously and mourning, saying thus to our Lord in my meaning, with full great dread: *Ah! good Lord, how might all be well, for the great hurt that is come, by sin, to the creature?* And here I desired, as far as I durst, to have some more open declaring wherewith I might be eased in this matter.

And to this our blessed Lord answered full meekly and with full lovely cheer, and shewed that Adam's sin was the most harm that ever was done, or ever shall be, to the world's end; and also He shewed that this [sin] is openly known in all Holy Church on earth. Furthermore He taught that I should behold the glorious Satisfaction: for this Amends-making is more pleasing to God and more worshipful, without comparison, than ever was the sin of Adam harmful. Then signifieth our blessed Lord thus in this teaching, that we should take heed to this: *For since I have made well the most harm, then it is my will that thou know thereby that I shall make well all that is less.*

CHAPTER XXX

"Two parts of Truth: the part that is open: our Saviour and our salvation;—and the part that is hid and shut up from us: all beside our salvation"

He gave me understanding of two parts [of truth]. The one part is our Saviour and our salvation. This blessed part is open and clear and fair and light, and plenteous,—for all mankind that is of good will, and shall be, is comprehended in this part. Hereto are we bounden of God, and drawn and counselled and taught inwardly by the Holy Ghost and outwardly by Holy Church in the same grace. In this willeth our Lord that we be occupied, joying in Him; for He enjoyeth in us. The more plenteously that we take of this, with reverence and meekness, the more thanks we earn of Him and the more speed to ourselves, thus— may we say—enjoying *our* part of our Lord. The other [part] is hid and shut up from us: that is to say, all that is beside our salvation. For it is our Lord's privy counsel, and it belongeth to the royal lordship of God to have His privy counsel in peace, and it belongeth to His servant, for obedience and reverence, not to learn wholly His counsel. Our Lord hath pity and compassion on us for that some creatures make themselves so busy therein; and I am sure if we knew how much we should please Him and ease ourselves by leaving it, we would. The saints that be in Heaven, they will to know nothing but that which our Lord willeth to shew them: and also their charity and their desire is ruled after the will of our Lord: and thus ought we to will, like to them. Then shall we nothing will nor desire but the will of our Lord, as they do: for we are all one in God's seeing.

And here was I learned that we shall trust and rejoice only in our Saviour, blessed Jesus, for all thing.

CHAPTER XXXI

"The Spiritual Thirst (which was in Him from without beginning) is
desire in Him as long as we be in need, drawing us up to His Bliss"

And thus our good Lord answered to all the questions and doubts that
I might make, saying full comfortably: *I may make all thing well, I can
make all thing well, I will make all thing well, and I shall make all
thing well; and thou shalt see thyself that all manner of thing shall be
well.*

In that He saith, *I may*, I understand [it] for the Father; and in that He
saith, *I can*, I understand [it] for the Son; and where He saith, *I will*, I
understand [it] for the Holy Ghost; and where He saith, *I shall*, I
understand [it] for the unity of the blessed Trinity: three Persons and
one Truth; and where He saith, *Thou shalt see thyself*, I understand
the oneing of all mankind that shall be saved unto the blessed Trinity.
And in these five words God willeth we be enclosed in rest and in
peace.

Thus shall the Spiritual Thirst of Christ have an end. For this is the
Spiritual Thirst of Christ: the love-longing that lasteth, and ever shall,
till we see that sight on Doomsday. For we that shall be saved and
shall be Christ's joy and His bliss, some be yet here and some be to
come, and so shall some be, unto that day. Therefore this is His thirst
and love-longing, to have us altogether whole in Him, to His bliss,—
as to my sight. For we be not now as fully whole in Him as we shall be
then.

For we know in our Faith, and also it was shewed in all [the
Revelations] that Christ Jesus is both God and man. And anent the
Godhead, He is Himself highest bliss, and was, from without
beginning, and shall be, without end: which endless bliss may never
be heightened nor lowered in itself. For this was plenteously seen in
every Shewing, and specially in the Twelfth, where He saith: *I am that
[which] is highest.* And anent Christ's Manhood, it is known in our
Faith, and also [it was] shewed, that He, with the virtue of Godhead,
for love, to bring us to His bliss suffered pains and passions, and died.
And these be the works of Christ's Manhood wherein He rejoiceth;
and that shewed He in the Ninth Revelation, where He saith: *It is a
joy and bliss and endless pleasing to me that ever I suffered Passion*

for thee. And this is the bliss of Christ's *works*, and thus he signifieth where He saith in that same Shewing: we be His bliss, we be His meed, we be His worship, we be His crown.

For anent that Christ is our Head, He is glorified and impassible; and anent His Body in which all His members are knit, He is not yet fully glorified nor all impassible. Therefore the same desire and thirst that He had upon the Cross (which desire, longing, and thirst, as to my sight, was in Him from without beginning) the same hath He yet, and shall [have] unto the time that the last soul that shall be saved is come up to His bliss.

For as verily as there is a property in God of ruth and pity, so verily there is a property in God of thirst and longing. (And of the virtue of this longing in Christ, *we* have to long again to Him: without which no soul cometh to Heaven.) And this property of longing and thirst cometh of the endless Goodness of God, even as the property of pity cometh of His endless Goodness. And though longing and pity are two sundry properties, as to my sight, in this standeth the point of the Spiritual Thirst: which is *desire in Him as long as we be in need*, drawing us up to His bliss. And all this was seen in the Shewing of Compassion: for that shall cease on Doomsday.

Thus He hath ruth and compassion on us, and He hath longing to have us; but His wisdom and His love suffereth not the end to come till the best time.

CHAPTER XXXII

"There be deeds evil done in our sight, and so great harms taken, that it seemeth to us that it were impossible that ever it should come to good end." "That Great Deed ordained ... by which our Lord God shall make all things well"

One time our good Lord said: *All thing shall be well*; and another time he said: *Thou shalt see thyself that all* manner *[of] thing shall be well*; and in these two [sayings] the soul took sundry understandings.

One was that He willeth we know that not only He taketh heed to noble things and to great, but also to little and to small, to low and to simple, to one and to other. And so meaneth He in that He saith: All manner of things *shall be well*. For He willeth we know that the least thing shall not be forgotten.

Another understanding is this, that there be deeds evil done in our sight, and so great harms taken, that it seemeth to us that it were impossible that ever it should come to good end. And upon this we look, sorrowing and mourning therefor, so that we cannot resign us unto the blissful beholding of God as we should do. And the cause of this is that the use of our reason is now so blind, so low, and so simple, that we cannot know that high marvellous Wisdom, the Might and the Goodness of the blissful Trinity. And thus signifieth He when He saith: Thou shalt see thyself *if all manner of things shall be well*. As if He said: *Take now heed faithfully and trustingly, and at the last end thou shalt verily see it in fulness of joy*.

And thus in these same five words aforesaid: *I may make all things well*, etc., I understand a mighty comfort of all the works of our Lord God that are yet to come. There is a Deed the which the blessed Trinity shall do in the last Day, as to my sight, and when the Deed shall be, and how it shall be done, is unknown of all creatures that are beneath Christ, and shall be till when it is done.

["The Goodness and the Love of our Lord God will that we wit [know] that it shall be; And the Might and the Wisdom of him by the same Love will hill [conceal] it, and hide it from us what it shall be, and how it shall be done."]

And the cause why He willeth that we know [this Deed shall be], is for that He would have us the more eased in our soul and [the more] set at peace in love—leaving the beholding of all troublous things that might keep us back from true enjoying of Him. This is that Great Deed ordained of our Lord God from without beginning, treasured and hid in His blessed breast, only known to Himself: by which He shall make all things well.

For like as the blissful Trinity made all things of nought, right so the same blessed Trinity shall make well all that is not well.

And in this sight I marvelled greatly and beheld our Faith, marvelling thus: Our Faith is grounded in God's word, and it belongeth to our Faith that we believe that God's word shall be saved in all things; and one point of our Faith is that many creatures shall be condemned: as angels that fell out of Heaven for pride, which be now fiends; and man in earth that dieth out of the Faith of Holy Church: that is to say, they that be heathen men; and also man that hath received Christendom and liveth unchristian life and so dieth out of charity: all these shall be condemned to hell without end, as Holy Church teacheth me to believe. And all this [so] standing, methought it was impossible that all manner of things should be well, as our Lord shewed in the same time.

And as to this I had no other answer in Shewing of our Lord God but this: *That which is impossible to thee is not impossible to me: I shall save my word in all things and I shall make all things well.* Thus I was taught, by the grace of God, that I should steadfastly hold me in the Faith as I had aforehand understood, [and] therewith that I should firmly believe that all things shall be well, as our Lord shewed in the same time.

For this is the Great Deed that our Lord shall do, in which Deed He shall save His word and He shall make all well that is not well. How it shall be done there is no creature beneath Christ that knoweth it, nor shall know it till it is done; according to the understanding that I took of our Lord's meaning in this time.

CHAPTER XXXIII

"It is God's will that we have great regard to all His deeds that He hath done, but evermore it needeth us to leave the beholding what the Deed shall be"

And yet in this I desired, as [far] as I durst, that I might have full sight of Hell and Purgatory. But it was not my meaning to make proof of anything that belongeth to the Faith: for I believed soothfastly that Hell and Purgatory is for the same end that Holy Church teacheth, but my meaning was that I might have seen, for learning in all things that belong to my Faith: whereby I might live the more to God's worship and to my profit.

But for [all] my desire, I could [see] of this right nought, save as it is aforesaid in the First Shewing, where I saw that the devil is reproved of God and endlessly condemned. In which sight I understood as to all creatures that are of the devil's condition in this life, and therein end, that there is no more mention made of them afore God and all His Holy than of the devil,—notwithstanding that they be of mankind—whether they be christened or not.

For though the Revelation was made of goodness in which was made little mention of evil, yet I was not drawn thereby from any point of the Faith that Holy Church teacheth me to believe. For I had sight of the Passion of Christ in diverse Shewings,—the First, the Second, the Fifth, and the Eighth,—wherein I had in part a feeling of the sorrow of our Lady, and of His true friends that saw Him in pain; but I saw not so properly specified the Jews that did Him to death. Notwithstanding I knew in my Faith that they were accursed and condemned without end, saving those that converted, by grace. And I was strengthened and taught generally to keep me in the Faith in every point, and in all as I had before understood: hoping that I was therein with the mercy and the grace of God; desiring and praying in my purpose that I might continue therein unto my life's end.

And it is God's will that we have great regard to all His deeds that He hath done, but evermore it needeth us to leave the beholding what the Deed shall be. And let us desire to be like our brethren which be saints in Heaven, that will right nought but God's will and are well pleased both with hiding and with shewing. For I saw soothly in our Lord's teaching, the more we busy us to know His secret counsels in this or any other thing, the farther shall we be from the knowing thereof.

CHAPTER XXXIV

"All that is speedful for us to learn and to know, full courteously will our Lord shew us"

Our Lord God shewed two manner of secret things. One is this great Secret [Counsel] with all the privy points that belong thereto: and these secret things He willeth we should know [as *being*, but as] *hid* until the time that He will clearly shew them to us. The other are the secret things that He willeth to make open and known to us; for He would have us understand that it is His will that we should know them. They are secrets to us not only for that He willeth that they be secrets to us, but they are secrets to us for our blindness and our ignorance; and thereof He hath great ruth, and therefore He will Himself make them more open to us, whereby we may know Him and love Him and cleave to Him. For all that is speedful for us to learn and to know, full courteously will our Lord shew us: and [of] that is this [Shewing], with all the preaching and teaching of Holy Church.

God shewed full great pleasance that He hath in all men and women that mightily and meekly and with all their will take the preaching and teaching of Holy Church. For it is His Holy Church: He is the Ground, He is the Substance, He is the Teaching, He is the Teacher, He is the End, He is the Meed for which every kind soul travaileth.

And *this* [of the Shewing] is [made] known, and shall be known to every soul to which the Holy Ghost declareth it. And I hope truly that all those that seek this, He shall speed: for they seek God.

All this that I have now told, and more that I shall tell after, is comforting against sin. For in the Third Shewing when I saw that God doeth all that is done, I saw no sin: and then I saw that all *is* well. But when God shewed me for sin, then said He: *All* shall *be well.*

CHAPTER XXXV

"I desired to learn assuredly as to a certain creature that I loved.... It is more worship to God to behold Him in *all* than in any special thing"

And when God Almighty had shewed so plenteously and joyfully of His Goodness, I desired to learn assuredly as to a certain creature that I loved, if it should continue in good living, which I hoped by the grace of God was begun. And in this desire for a *singular* Shewing, it seemed that I hindered myself: for I was not taught in this time. And then was I answered in my reason, as it were by a friendly intervenor: *Take it* generally, *and behold the graciousness of the Lord God as He sheweth to thee: for it is more worship to God to behold Him in all than in any special thing.* And therewith I learned that it is more worship to God to know all-thing in general, than to take pleasure in any special thing. And if I should do wisely according to this teaching, I should not only be glad for nothing in special, but I should not be greatly distressed for no manner of thing: for All *shall be well*. For the fulness of joy is to behold God in *all*: for by the same blessed Might, Wisdom, and Love, that He made all-thing, to the same end our good Lord leadeth it continually, and thereto Himself shall bring it; and when it is time we shall see it. And the ground of this was shewed in the First [Revelation], and more openly in the Third, where it saith: *I saw God in a point*.

All that our Lord doeth is rightful, and that which He suffereth is worshipful: and in these two is comprehended good and ill: for all that is good our Lord doeth, and that which is evil our Lord suffereth. I say not that any evil is worshipful, but I say the sufferance of our Lord God is worshipful: whereby His Goodness shall be known, without end, in His marvellous meekness and mildness, by the working of mercy and grace.

Rightfulness is that thing that is so good that [it] may not be better than it is. For God Himself is very Rightfulness, and all His works are done rightfully as they are ordained from without beginning by His high Might, His high Wisdom, His high Goodness. And right as He ordained unto the best, right so He worketh continually, and leadeth it to the same end; and He is ever full-pleased with Himself and with all His works. And the beholding of this blissful accord is full sweet to the soul that seeth by grace. All the souls that shall be saved in Heaven without end be made rightful in the sight of God, and by His own goodness: in which rightfulness we are endlessly kept, and marvellously, above all creatures.

And *Mercy* is a working that cometh of the goodness of God, and it shall last in working all along, as sin is suffered to pursue rightful souls. And when sin hath no longer leave to pursue, then shall the working of mercy cease, and then shall all be brought to rightfulness and therein stand without end.

And by His sufferance we fall; and in His blissful Love with His Might and His Wisdom we are kept; and by mercy and grace we are raised to manifold more joys.

Thus in Rightfulness and Mercy He willeth to be known and loved, now and without end. And the soul that wisely beholdeth it in grace, it is well pleased with both, and endlessly enjoyeth.

CHAPTER XXXVI

"My sin shall not hinder His Goodness working.... A deed shall be
done—as we come to Heaven—and it may be known here in part;—
though it be truly taken for the general Man, yet it excludeth not the
special. For what our good Lord will do by His poor creatures, it is
now unknown to me"

Our Lord God shewed that a deed shall be done, and Himself shall do
it, and I shall do nothing but sin, and my sin shall not hinder His
Goodness working. And I saw that the beholding of this is a heavenly
joy in a fearing soul which evermore kindly by grace desireth God's
will. This deed shall be begun here, and it shall be worshipful to God
and plenteously profitable to His lovers in earth; and ever as we come
to Heaven we shall see it in marvellous joy, and it shall last thus in
working unto the last Day; and the worship and the bliss of it shall last
in Heaven afore God and all His Holy [ones] for ever.

Thus was this deed seen and understood in our Lord's signifying: and
the cause why He shewed it is to make us rejoice in Him and in all His
works. When I saw His Shewing continued, I understood that it was
shewed for a great thing that was for to come, which thing God
shewed that He Himself should do it: which deed hath these
properties aforesaid. And this shewed He well blissfully, signifying
that I should take it myself faithfully and trustingly.

But what this deed should be was kept secret from me.

And in this I saw that He willeth not that we dread to know the things
that He sheweth: He sheweth them because He would have us know
them; by which knowing He would have us love Him and have
pleasure and endlessly enjoy in Him. For the great love that He hath
to us He sheweth us all that is worshipful and profitable for the time.
And the things that He will now have privy, yet of His great goodness
He sheweth them *close*: in which shewing He willeth that we believe
and understand that we shall see the same verily in His endless bliss.
Then ought we to rejoice in Him for all that He sheweth and all that
He hideth; and if we steadily and meekly do thus, we shall find therein
great ease; and endless thanks we shall have of Him therefor.

And this is the understanding of this word:—That it shall be done for me, meaneth that it shall be done for the general Man: that is to say, all that shall be saved. It shall be worshipful and marvellous and plenteous, and God Himself shall do it; and this shall be the highest joy that may be, to behold the deed that God Himself shall do, and man shall do right nought but sin. Then signifieth our Lord God thus, as if He said: *Behold and see! Here hast thou matter of meekness, here hast thou matter of love, here hast thou matter to make nought of thyself, here hast thou matter to enjoy in me;—and, for my love, enjoy [thou] in me: for of all things, therewith mightest thou please me most.*

And as long as we are in this life, what time that we by our folly turn us to the beholding of the reproved, tenderly our Lord God toucheth us and blissfully calleth us, saying in our soul: *Let be all thy love, my dearworthy child: turn thee to me—I am enough to thee—and enjoy in thy Saviour and in thy salvation.* And that this is our Lord's working in us, I am sure the soul that hath understanding therein by grace shall see it and feel it.

And though it be so that this deed be truly taken for the general Man, yet it excludeth not the special. For what our good Lord will do by His poor creatures, it is now unknown to me.

But this deed and that other aforesaid, they are not both one but two sundry. This deed shall be done sooner (and that [time] shall be as we come to Heaven), and to whom our Lord giveth it, it may be known here in part. But that Great Deed aforesaid shall neither be known in Heaven nor earth till it is done.

And moreover He gave special understanding and teaching of working of miracles, as thus:—*It is known that I have done miracles here afore, many and diverse, high and marvellous, worshipful and great. And so as I have done, I do now continually, and shall do in coming of time.*

It is known that afore miracles come sorrow and anguish and tribulation; and that is for that we should know our own feebleness and our mischiefs that we are fallen in by sin, to meeken us and make us to dread God and cry for help and grace. Miracles come after that, and they come of the high Might, Wisdom, and Goodness of God, shewing His virtue and the joys of Heaven so far at it may be in this passing life: and that to strengthen our faith and to increase our hope, in charity. Wherefore it pleaseth Him to be known and worshipped in miracles. Then signifieth He thus: He willeth that we be not borne over low for sorrow and tempests that fall to us: for it hath ever so been afore miracle-coming.

CHAPTER XXXVII

"In every soul that shall be saved is a Godly Will that never assented to sin, nor ever shall."—"For failing of Love on our part, therefore is all our travail"

God brought to my mind that I should sin. And for pleasance that I had in beholding of Him, I attended not readily to that shewing; and our Lord full mercifully abode, and gave me grace to attend. And this shewing I took singularly to myself; but by all the gracious comfort that followeth, as ye shall see, I was learned to take it for all mine even-Christians: *all in general and nothing in special*: though our Lord shewed me that I should sin, by me alone is understood all.

And therein I conceived a soft dread. And to this our Lord answered: *I keep thee full surely*. This word was said with more love and secureness and spiritual keeping than I can or may tell. For as it was shewed that [I] should sin, right so was the comfort shewed: secureness and keeping for all mine even-Christians.

What may make me more to love mine even-Christians than to see in God that He loveth all that shall be saved as it were all one soul?

For in every soul that shall be saved is a Godly Will that never assented to sin, nor ever shall. Right as there is a beastly will in the lower part that may will no good, right so there is a Godly Will in the higher part, which will is so good that it may never will evil, but ever good. And therefore we are that which He loveth and endlessly we do that which Him pleaseth.

This shewed our Lord in [shewing] the wholeness of love that we stand in, in His sight: yea, that He loveth us now as well while we are here, as He shall do while we are there afore His blessed face. But for failing of love on our part, therefore is all our travail.

CHAPTER XXXVIII

In Heaven "the token of sin is turned to worship."—*Examples thereof*

Also God shewed that sin shall be no shame to man, but worship. For right as to every sin is answering a pain by truth, right so for every sin, to the same soul is given a bliss by love: right as diverse sins are punished with diverse pains according as they be grievous, right so shall they be rewarded with diverse joys in Heaven according as they have been painful and sorrowful to the soul in earth. For the soul that shall come to Heaven is precious to God, and the place so worshipful that the goodness of God suffereth never that soul to sin that shall come there without that the which sin shall be rewarded; and it is made known without end, and blissfully restored by overpassing worship.

For in this Sight mine understanding was lifted up into Heaven, and then God brought merrily to my mind David, and others in the Old Law without number; and in the New Law He brought to my mind first Mary Magdalene, Peter and Paul, and those of Inde; and Saint John of Beverley; and others also without number: how they are known in the Church in earth with their sins, and it is to them no shame, but all is turned for them to worship. And therefore our courteous Lord sheweth [it thus] for them here in part like as it is there in fulness: for there the token of sin is turned to worship.

And Saint John of Beverley, our Lord shewed him full highly, in comfort to us for homeliness; and brought to my mind how he is a dear neighbour, and of our knowing. And God called him *Saint John of Beverley* plainly as we do, and that with a most glad sweet cheer, shewing that he is a full high saint in Heaven in His sight, and a blissful. And with this he made mention that in his youth and in his tender age he was a dearworthy servant to God, greatly God loving and dreading, and yet God suffered him to fall, mercifully keeping him that he perished not, nor lost no time. And afterward God raised him to manifold more grace, and by the contrition and meekness that he had in his living, God hath given him in Heaven manifold joys, overpassing that [which] he should have had if he had not fallen. And that this is sooth, God sheweth in earth with plenteous miracles doing about his body continually.

And all this was to make us glad and merry in love.

CHAPTER XXXIX

"Sin is the sharpest scourge.... By contrition we are made clean, by
compassion we are made ready, and by true longing towards God we
are made worthy"

Sin is the sharpest scourge that any chosen soul may be smitten with:
which scourge thoroughly beateth man and woman, and maketh him
hateful in his own sight, so far forth that afterwhile he thinketh himself
he is not worthy but as to sink in hell,—till [that time] when contrition
taketh him by touching of the Holy Ghost, and turneth the bitterness
into hopes of God's mercy. And then He beginneth his wounds to heal,
and the soul to quicken [as it is] turned unto the life of Holy Church.
The Holy Ghost leadeth him to confession, with all his will to shew
his sins nakedly and truly, with great sorrow and great shame that he
hath defouled the fair image of God. Then receiveth he penance for
every sin [as] enjoined by his doomsman that is grounded in Holy
Church by the teaching of the Holy Ghost. And this is one meekness
that greatly pleaseth God; and also bodily sickness of God's sending,
and also sorrow and shame from without, and reproof, and despite of
this world, with all manner of grievance and temptations that we be
cast in, bodily and ghostly.

Full preciously our Lord keepeth us when it seemeth to us that we are
near forsaken and cast away for our sin and because we have
deserved it. And because of meekness that we get hereby, we are
raised well-high in God's sight by His grace, with so great contrition,
and also compassion, and true longing to God. Then they be suddenly
delivered from sin and from pain, and taken up to bliss, and made
even high saints.

By contrition we are made clean, by compassion we are made ready,
and by true longing toward God we are made worthy. These are three
means, as I understand, whereby that all souls come to heaven: that is
to say, that have been sinners in earth and shall be saved: for by these
three medicines it behoveth that every soul be healed. Though the
soul be healed, his wounds are seen afore God,—not as wounds but
as worships. And so on the contrary-wise, as we be punished here
with sorrow and penance, we shall be rewarded in heaven by the

courteous love of our Lord God Almighty, who willeth that none that come there lose his travail in any degree. For He [be]holdeth sin as sorrow and pain to His lovers, to whom He assigneth no blame, for love. The meed that we shall receive shall not be little, but it shall be high, glorious, and worshipful. And so shall shame be turned to worship and more joy.

But our courteous Lord willeth not that His servants despair, for often nor for grievous falling: for our falling hindereth not Him to love us. Peace and love are ever in us, being and working; but we be not alway in peace and in love. But He willeth that we take heed thus that He is Ground of all our whole life in love; and furthermore that He is our everlasting Keeper and mightily defendeth us against our enemies, that be full fell and fierce upon us;—and so much our need is the more for [that] we give them occasion by our falling.

CHAPTER XL

"True love teacheth us that we should hate sin only for love." "To me was shewed no harder hell than sin." "God willeth that we endlessly hate the sin and endlessly love the soul, as God loveth it"

This is a sovereign friendship of our courteous Lord that He keepeth us so tenderly while we be in sin; and furthermore He toucheth us full privily and sheweth us our sin by the sweet light of mercy and grace. But when we see our self so foul, then ween we that God were wroth with us for our sin, and then are we stirred of the Holy Ghost by contrition unto prayer and desire for the amending of our life with all our mights, to slacken the wrath of God, unto the time we find a rest in soul and a softness in conscience. Then hope we that God hath forgiven us our sins: and it is truth. And then sheweth our courteous Lord Himself to the soul—well-merrily and with glad cheer—with friendly welcoming as if it had been in pain and in prison, saying sweetly thus: *My darling I am glad thou art come to me: in all thy wo I have ever been with thee; and now seest thou my loving and we be oned in bliss.* Thus are sins forgiven by mercy and grace, and our soul is worshipfully received in joy like as it shall be when it cometh to Heaven, as oftentimes as it cometh by the gracious working of the Holy Ghost and the virtue of Christ's Passion.

Here understand I in truth that all manner of things are made ready for us by the great goodness of God, so far forth that what time we be ourselves in peace and charity, we be verily saved. But because we may not have this in fulness while we are here, therefore it falleth to us evermore to live in sweet prayer and lovely longing with our Lord Jesus. For He longeth ever to bring us to the fulness of joy; as it is aforesaid, where He sheweth the Spiritual Thirst.

But now if any man or woman because of all this spiritual comfort that is aforesaid, be stirred by folly to say or to think: *If this be true, then were it good to sin [so as] to have the more meed*,—or else to charge the less [guilt] to sin,—beware of this stirring: for verily if it come it is untrue, and of the enemy of the same true love that teacheth us that we should hate sin only for love. I am sure by mine own feeling, the more that any kind soul seeth this in the courteous love of our Lord God, the lother he is to sin and the more he is ashamed. For if afore us were laid [together] all the pains in Hell and in Purgatory and in Earth—death and other—, and [by itself] sin, we should rather choose all that pain than sin. For sin is so vile and so greatly to be hated that it may be likened to no pain which is not sin. And to me was shewed no harder hell than sin. For a kind soul hath no hell but sin.

And [when] we give our intent to love and meekness, by the working of mercy and grace we are made all fair and clean. As mighty and as wise as God is to save men, so willing He is. For Christ Himself is [the] ground of all the laws of Christian men, and He taught us to do good against ill: here may we see that He is Himself this charity, and doeth to us as He teacheth us to do. For He willeth that we be like Him in wholeness of endless love to ourself and to our even-Christians: no more than His love is broken to us for our sin, no more willeth He that our love be broken to ourself and to our even-Christians: but [that we] endlessly hate the sin and endlessly love the soul, as God loveth it. Then shall we hate sin like as God hateth it, and love the soul as God loveth it. And this word that He said is an endless comfort: *I keep thee securely*.

THE FOURTEENTH REVELATION.

CHAPTER XLI

"I am the Ground of thy beseeching." "Also to prayer belongeth
thanking"

After this our Lord shewed concerning Prayer. In which Shewing I
see two conditions in our Lord's signifying: one is rightfulness,
another is sure trust.

But yet oftentimes our trust is not full: for we are not sure that God
heareth us, as we think because of our unworthiness, and because we
feel right nought, (for we are as barren and dry oftentimes after our
prayers as we were afore); and this, in our feeling our folly, is cause of
our weakness. For thus have I felt in myself.

And all this brought our Lord suddenly to my mind, and shewed these
words, and said: *I am Ground of thy beseeching: first it is my will that
thou have it; and after, I make thee to will it; and after, I make thee to
beseech it and thou beseechest it. How should it then be that thou
shouldst not have thy beseeching?*

And thus in the first reason, with the three that follow, our good Lord
sheweth a mighty comfort, as it may be seen in the same words. And
in the first reason,—where He saith: *And thou beseechest it*, there He
sheweth [His] full great pleasance, and endless meed that He will give
us for our beseeching. And in the second reason, where He saith: *How
should it then be?* etc., this was said for an impossible [thing]. For it is
most impossible that we should beseech mercy and grace, and not
have it. For everything that our good Lord maketh us to beseech,
Himself hath ordained it to us from without beginning. Here may we
see that our beseeching is not cause of God's goodness; and that
shewed He soothfastly in all these sweet words when He saith: *I am
[the] Ground.*—And our good Lord willeth that this be known of His
lovers in earth; and the more that we know [it] the more should we
beseech, if it be wisely taken; and so is our Lord's meaning.

Beseeching is a true, gracious, lasting will of the soul, oned and
fastened into the will of our Lord by the sweet inward work of the
Holy Ghost. Our Lord Himself, He is the first receiver of our prayer,

as to my sight, and taketh it full thankfully and highly enjoying; and He sendeth it up above and setteth it in the Treasure, where it shall never perish. It is there afore God with all His Holy continually received, ever speeding [the help of] our needs; and when we shall receive our bliss it shall be given us for a degree of joy, with endless worshipful thanking from Him.

Full glad and merry is our Lord of our prayer; and He looketh thereafter and He willeth to have it because with His grace He maketh us like to Himself in condition as we are in kind: and so is His blissful will. Therefore He saith thus: *Pray inwardly, though thee thinketh it savour thee not: for it is profitable, though thou feel not, though thou see nought; yea, though thou think thou canst not. For in dryness and in barrenness, in sickness and in feebleness, then is thy prayer well-pleasant to me, though thee thinketh it savour thee nought but little. And so is all thy believing prayer in my sight.* For the meed and the endless thanks that He will give us, *therefor* He is covetous to have us pray continually in His sight. God accepteth the goodwill and the travail of His servant, howsoever we feel: wherefore it pleaseth Him that we work both in our prayers and in good living, by His help and His grace, reasonably with discretion keeping our powers [turned] to Him, till when that we have Him that we seek, in fulness of joy: that is, Jesus. And that shewed He in the Fifteenth [Revelation], farther on, in this word: *Thou shalt have me to thy meed.*

And also to prayer belongeth thanking. Thanking is a true inward knowing, with great reverence and lovely dread turning ourselves with all our mights unto the working that our good Lord stirreth us to, enjoying and thanking inwardly. And sometimes, for plenteousness it breaketh out with voice, and saith: *Good Lord, I thank Thee! Blessed mayst Thou be!* And sometime when the heart is dry and feeleth not, or else by temptation of our enemy,—then it is driven by reason and by grace to cry upon our Lord with voice, rehearing His blessed Passion and His great Goodness; and the virtue of our Lord's word turneth into the soul and quickeneth the heart and entereth it by His grace into true working, and maketh it pray right blissfully. And truly to enjoy our Lord, it is a full blissful thanking in His sight.

CHAPTER XLII

"Prayer is a right understanding of that fulness of joy that is to come, with accordant longing and sure trust"

Our Lord God willeth that we have true understanding, and specially in three things that belong to our prayer. The first is: *by whom and how that our prayer springeth. By whom*, He sheweth when He saith: *I am [the] Ground*; and *how*, by His Goodness: for He saith first: *It is my will.* The second is: *in what manner and how we should use our prayer*; and that is that our will be turned unto the will of our Lord, enjoying: and so meaneth He when He saith: *I make thee to will it.* The third is that we should know *the fruit and the end of our prayers*: that is, that we be oned and like to our Lord in all things; and to this intent and for this end was all this lovely lesson shewed. And He will help us, and we shall make it so as He saith Himself;—Blessed may He be!

For this is our Lord's will, that our prayer and our trust be both alike large. For if we trust not as much as we pray, we do not full worship to our Lord in our prayer, and also we tarry and pain our self. The cause is, as I believe, that we know not truly that our Lord is [the] Ground on whom our prayer springeth; and also that we know not that it is given us by the grace of His love. For if we knew this, it would make us to trust to have, of our Lord's gift, all that we desire. For I am sure that no man asketh mercy and grace with true meaning, but if mercy and grace be first given to him.

But sometimes it cometh to our mind that we have prayed long time, and yet we think to ourselves that we have not our asking. But herefor should we not be in heaviness. For I am sure, by our Lord's signifying, that either we abide a better time, or more grace, or a better gift. He willeth that we have true knowing in Himself that He is Being; and in this knowing He willeth that our understanding be grounded, with all our mights and all our intent and all our meaning; and in this ground He willeth that we take our place and our dwelling, and by the gracious light of Himself He willeth that we have understanding of the things that follow. The first is our noble and excellent making; the second, our precious and dearworthy again-buying; the third, all-thing that He hath made beneath us, [He hath made] to serve us, and for our love keepeth it. Then signifieth He thus, as if He said: *Behold and see that I have done all this before thy prayers; and now thou art, and prayest me.* And thus He signifieth that it belongeth to us to learn that the greatest deeds be [already] done, as Holy Church teacheth; and in the beholding of this, with thanking, we ought to pray for the deed that is now in doing: and that is, that He rule and guide us, to His worship, in this life, and bring us to His bliss. And therefor He hath done all.

Then signifieth He thus: that we [should] see that He doeth it, and that we [should] pray therefor. For the one is not enough. For if we pray and see not that He doeth it, it maketh us heavy and doubtful; and that is not His worship. And if we see that He doeth, and we pray not, we do not our debt, and so may it not be: that is to say, so is it not [the thing that is] in His beholding. But to see that He doeth it, and to pray forthwithal,—so is he worshipped and we sped. All-thing that our Lord hath ordained to do, it is His will that we pray therefor, either in special or in general. And the joy and the bliss that it is to Him, and the thanks and the worship that we shall have therefor, it passeth the understanding of creatures, as to my sight.

For prayer is a right understanding of that fulness of joy that is to come, with well-longing and sure trust. Failing of our bliss that we be kindly ordained to, maketh us to long; true understanding and love, with sweet mind in our Saviour, graciously maketh us to trust. And in these two workings our Lord beholdeth us continually: for it is our due part, and His Goodness may no less assign to us.

Thus it belongeth to us to do our diligence; and when we have done it, then shall us yet think that [it] is nought,—and sooth it is. But if we do as we can, and ask, in truth, for mercy and grace, all that faileth us we shall find in Him. And thus signifieth He where He saith: *I am Ground of thy beseeching.* And thus in this blessed word, with the Shewing, I saw a full overcoming against all our weakness and all our doubtful dreads.

CHAPTER XLIII

"Prayer uniteth the soul to God"

Prayer oneth the soul to God. For though the soul be ever like to God in kind and substance, restored by grace, it is often unlike in condition, by sin on man's part. Then is prayer a witness that the soul willeth as God willeth; and it comforteth the conscience and enableth man to grace. And thus He teacheth us to pray, and mightily to trust that we shall have it. For He beholdeth us in love and would make us partners of His good deed, and therefore He stirreth us to pray for that which it pleaseth him to do. For which prayer and good will, that we have of His gift, He will reward us and give us endless meed.

And this was shewed in this word: *And thou beseechest it.* In this word God shewed so great pleasance and so great content, as though He were much beholden to us for every good deed that we do (and yet it is *He* that doeth it) because that we beseech Him mightily to do all things that seem to Him good: as if He said: *What might then please me more than to beseech me, mightily, wisely, and earnestly, to do that thing that I shall do?*

And thus the soul by prayer accordeth to God.

But when our courteous Lord of His grace sheweth Himself to our soul, we have that [which] we desire. And then we see not, for the time, what we should more pray, but all our intent with all our might is set wholly to the beholding of Him. And this is an high unperceivable prayer, as to my sight: for all the cause wherefor we pray it, is oned into the sight and beholding of Him to whom we pray; marvellously enjoying with reverent dread, and with so great sweetness and delight in Him that we can pray right nought but as He stirreth us, for the time. And well I wot, the more the soul seeth of God, the more it desireth Him by His grace.

But when we see Him not so, then feel we need and cause to pray, because of failing, for enabling of our self, to Jesus. For when the soul is tempested, troubled, and left to itself by unrest, then it is time to pray, for to make itself pliable and obedient to God. (But the soul by no manner of prayer maketh God pliant to it: for He is ever alike in love.)

And this I saw: that what time we see needs wherefor we pray, then our *good Lord followeth us*, helping our desire; and when we of His special grace plainly behold Him, seeing none other needs, then *we follow Him* and He draweth us unto Him by love. For I saw and felt that His marvellous and plentiful Goodness fulfilleth all our powers; and therewith I saw that His continuant working in all manner of things is done so goodly, so wisely, and so mightily, that it overpasseth all our imagining, and all that we can ween and think; and then we can do no more but behold Him, enjoying, with an high, mighty desire to be all oned unto Him,—centred to His dwelling,—and enjoy in His loving and delight in His goodness.

And then shall we, with His sweet grace, in our own meek continuant prayer come unto Him now in this life by many privy touchings of sweet spiritual sights and feeling, measured to us as our simpleness may bear it. And this is wrought, and shall be, by the grace of the Holy Ghost, so long till we shall die in longing, for love. And then shall we all come into our Lord, our Self clearly knowing, and God fully having; and we shall endlessly be all had in God: Him verily seeing and fully feeling, Him spiritually hearing, and Him delectably in-breathing, and [of] Him sweetly drinking.

And then shall we see God face to face, homely and fully. The creature that is made shall see and endlessly behold God which is the Maker. For thus may no man see God and live after, that is to say, in this deadly life. But when He of His special grace will shew Himself here, He strengtheneth the creature above its self, and He measureth the Shewing, after His own will, as it is profitable for the time.

ANENT CERTAIN POINTS IN THE FOREGOING FOURTEEN REVELATIONS

CHAPTER XLIV

"God is endless, sovereign Truth,—Wisdom,—Love, not-made; and man's Soul is a creature in God which hath the same properties made"

God shewed in all the Revelations, oftentimes, that man worketh evermore His will and His worship lastingly without any stinting. And *what* this work is, was shewed in the First, and that in a marvellous example: for it was shewed in the working of the soul of our blissful Lady, Saint Mary: [that is, the working of] Truth and Wisdom. And *how* [it is done] I hope by the grace of the Holy Ghost I shall tell, as I saw.

Truth seeth God, and Wisdom beholdeth God, and of these two cometh the third: that is, a holy marvellous delight in God; which is Love. Where Truth and Wisdom are verily, there is Love verily, coming of them both. And all of God's making: for He is endless sovereign Truth, endless sovereign Wisdom, endless sovereign Love, unmade; and man's Soul is a creature in God which hath the same properties *made*, and evermore it doeth that it was made for: it seeth God, it beholdeth God, and it loveth God. Whereof God enjoyeth in the creature; and the creature in God, endlessly marvelling.

In which marvelling he seeth his God, his Lord, his Maker so high, so great, and so good, in comparison with him that is made, that scarcely the creature seemeth ought to the self. But the clarity and the clearness of Truth and Wisdom maketh him to see and to bear witness that he is made for Love: in which God endlessly keepeth him.

CHAPTER XLV

"All heavenly things and all earthly things that belong to Heaven are comprehended in these two judgments"

God deemeth us [looking] upon our Nature-Substance, which is ever kept one in Him, whole and safe without end: and *this* doom is [because] of His rightfulness [in the which it is made and kept]. And man judgeth [looking] upon our changeable Sense-soul, which seemeth now one [thing], now other,—according as it taketh of the [higher or lower] parts,—and [is that which] showeth outward. And *this* wisdom [of man's judgment] is *mingled* [because of the diverse things it beholdeth]. For sometimes it is good and easy, and sometimes it is hard and grievous. And in as much as it is good and easy it belongeth to the rightfulness; and in as much as it is hard and grievous [by reason of the sin beheld, which sheweth in our Sense-soul,] our good Lord Jesus reformeth it by [the working in our Sense-soul of] mercy and grace through the virtue of His blessed Passion, and so bringeth it to the rightfulness.

And though these two [judgments] be thus accorded and oned, yet both shall be known in Heaven without end. The first doom, which is of God's rightfulness, is [because] of His high endless life [in our Substance]; and this is that fair sweet doom that was shewed in all the fair Revelation, in which I saw Him assign to us no manner of blame. But though this was sweet and delectable, yet in the beholding only of this, I could not be fully eased: and that was because of the doom of Holy Church, which I had afore understood and which was continually in my sight. And therefore by *this* doom methought I understood that sinners are worthy sometime of blame and wrath; but these two could I not see in God; and therefore my desire was more than I can or may tell. For the higher doom was shewed by God Himself in that same time, and therefore me behoved needs to take it; and the lower doom was learned me afore in Holy Church, and therefore I might in no way leave the lower doom. Then was this my desire: that I might see in God in what manner that which the doom of Holy Church teacheth is true in His sight, and how it belongeth to me verily to know it; whereby the two dooms might both be saved, so as it were worshipful to God and right way to me.

And to all this I had none other answer but a marvellous example of a lord and of a servant, as I shall tell after: and that full mistily shewed.

And yet I stand desiring, and will unto my end, that I might by grace know these two dooms as it belongeth to me. For all heavenly, and all earthly things that belong to Heaven, are comprehended in these two dooms. And the more understanding, by the gracious leading of the Holy Ghost, that we have of these two dooms, the more we shall see and know our failings. And ever the more that we see them, the more, of nature, by grace, we shall long to be fulfilled of endless joy and bliss. For we are made thereto, and our Nature-Substance is now blissful in God, and hath been since it was made, and shall be without end.

CHAPTER XLVI

"It is needful to see and to know that we are sinners: wherefore we deserve pain and wrath." "He is God: Good, Life, Truth, Love, Peace: His Clarity and His Unity suffereth Him not to be wroth"

But our passing life that we have here in our sense-soul knoweth not what our Self is. [And when we verily and clearly see and know what our Self is] then shall we verily and clearly see and know our Lord God in fulness of joy. And therefore it behoveth needs to be that the nearer we be to our bliss, the more we shall long [after it]: and that both by nature and by grace. We may have knowing of our Self in this life by continuant help and virtue of our high Nature. In which knowing we may exercise and grow, by forwarding and speeding of mercy and grace; but we may never fully know our Self until the last point: in which point this passing life and manner of pain and woe shall have an end. And therefore it belongeth properly to us, both by nature and by grace, to long and desire with all our mights to know our Self in fulness of endless joy.

And yet in all this time, from the beginning to the end, I had two manner of beholdings. The one was endless continuant love, with secureness of keeping, and blissful salvation,—for of this was all *the Shewing*. The other was of the common teaching of Holy Church, in which I was afore informed and grounded—and with all my will having in use and understanding. And the beholding of *this* went not from me: for by the Shewing I was not stirred nor led therefrom in no manner of point, but I had therein teaching to love it and find it good: whereby I might, by the help of our Lord and His grace, increase and rise to more heavenly knowing and higher loving.

And thus in all the Beholding methought it was needful to see and to know that we are sinners, and do many evils that we ought to leave, and leave many good deeds undone that we ought to do: wherefore we deserve pain and wrath. And notwithstanding all this, I saw soothfastly that our Lord was never wroth, nor ever shall be. For He is God: Good, Life, Truth, Love, Peace; His Clarity and His Unity suffereth Him not to be wroth. For I saw truly that it is against the property of His Might to be wroth, and against the property of His Wisdom, and against the property of His Goodness. God is the Goodness that may not be wroth, for He is not [other] but Goodness: our soul is oned to Him, unchangeable Goodness, and between God and our soul is neither wrath nor forgiveness in His sight. For our soul is so fully oned to God of His own Goodness that between God and our soul may be right nought.

And to this understanding was the soul led by love and drawn by might in every Shewing: *that it is thus* our good Lord shewed, and *how it is thus in truth of His great Goodness*. And He willeth that we desire to learn it—that is to say, as far as it belongeth to His creature to learn it. For all things that the simple soul understood, God willeth that they be shewed and [made] known. For the things that He will have privy, mightily and wisely Himself He hideth them, for love. For I saw in the same Shewing that much privity is hid, which may never be known until the time that God of His goodness hath made us worthy to see it; and therewith I am well-content, abiding our Lord's will in this high marvel. And now I yield me to my Mother, Holy Church, as a simple child oweth.

CHAPTER XLVII

"We fail oftentimes of the sight of Him, and anon we fall into our self, and then find we no feeling of right,—nought but contrariness that is in our self"

Two things belong to our soul as duty: the one is that we reverently marvel, the other that we meekly suffer, ever enjoying in God. For He would have us understand that we shall in short time see clearly in Himself all that we desire.

And notwithstanding all this, I beheld and marvelled greatly: *What is the mercy and forgiveness of God?* For by the teaching that I had afore,

I understood that the mercy of God should be the forgiveness of His wrath after the time that we have sinned. For methought that to a soul whose meaning and desire is to love, the wrath of God was harder than any other pain, and therefore I took that the forgiveness of His wrath should be one of the principal points of His mercy. But howsoever I might behold and desire, I could in no wise see this point in all the Shewing.

But how I understood and saw of the work of mercy, I shall tell somewhat, as God will give me grace. I understood this: Man is changeable in this life, and by frailty and overcoming falleth into sin: he is weak and unwise of himself, and also his will is overlaid. And in this time he is in tempest and in sorrow and woe; and the cause is blindness: for he seeth not God. For if he saw God continually, he should have no mischievous feeling, nor any manner of motion or yearning that serveth to sin.

Thus saw I, and felt in the same time; and methought that the sight and the feeling was high and plenteous and gracious in comparison with that which our common feeling is in this life; but yet I thought it was but small and low in comparison with the great desire that the soul hath to see God.

For I felt in me five manner of workings, which be these: Enjoying, mourning, desire, dread, and sure hope. Enjoying: for God gave me understanding and knowing that it was Himself that I saw; mourning: and that was for failing; desire: and that was I might see Him ever more and more, understanding and knowing that we shall never have full rest till we see Him verily and clearly in heaven; dread was: for it seemed to me in all that time that that sight should fail, and I be left to myself; sure hope was in the endless love: that I saw I should be kept by His mercy and brought to His bliss. And the joying in His sight with this sure hope of His merciful keeping made me to have feeling and comfort so that mourning and dread were not greatly painful. And yet in all this I beheld in the Shewing of God that this manner of sight may not be continuant in this life,—and that for His own worship and for increase of our endless joy. And therefore we fail oftentimes of the sight of Him, and anon we fall into our self, and then find we no feeling of right,—naught but contrariness that is in our self; and that of the elder root of our first sin, with all the sins that follow, of our contrivance. And in this we are in travail and tempest with feeling of sins, and of pain in many divers manners, spiritual and bodily, as it is known to us in this life.

CHAPTER XLVIII

"I beheld the property of Mercy, and I beheld the property of Grace: which have two manners of working in one love"

But our good Lord the Holy Ghost, which is endless life dwelling in our soul, full securely keepeth us; and worketh therein a peace and bringeth it to ease by grace, and accordeth it to God and maketh it pliant. And this is the mercy and the way that our Lord continually leadeth us in as long as we be here in this life which is changeable.

For I saw no wrath but on man's part; and that forgiveth He in us. For wrath is not else but a forwardness and a contrariness to peace and love; and either it cometh of failing of might, or of failing of wisdom, or of failing of goodness: which failing is not in God, but is on our part. For we by sin and wretchedness have in us a wretched and continuant contrariness to peace and to love. And that shewed He full often in His lovely Regard of Ruth and Pity. For the ground of mercy is love, and the working of mercy is our keeping in love. And this was shewed in such manner that I could not have perceived of the part of mercy but as it were alone in love; that is to say, as to my sight.

Mercy is a sweet gracious working in love, mingled with plenteous pity: for mercy worketh in keeping us, and mercy worketh turning to us all things to good. Mercy, by love, suffereth us to fail in measure and in as much as we fail, in so much we fall; and in as much as we fall, in so much we die: for it needs must be that we die in so much as we fail of the sight and feeling of God that is our life. Our failing is dreadful, our falling is shameful, and our dying is sorrowful: but in all this the sweet eye of pity and love is lifted never off us, nor the working of mercy ceaseth.

For I beheld the property of mercy, and I beheld the property of grace: which have two manners of working in one love. Mercy is a pitiful property which belongeth to the Motherhood in tender love; and grace is a worshipful property which belongeth to the royal Lordship in the same love. Mercy worketh: keeping, suffering, quickening, and healing; and all is tenderness of love. And grace worketh: raising, rewarding, endlessly overpassing that which our longing and our travail deserveth, spreading abroad and shewing the high plenteous largess of God's royal Lordship in His marvellous courtesy; and this is of the abundance of love. For grace worketh our dreadful failing into plenteous, endless solace; and grace worketh our shameful falling into high, worshipful rising; and grace worketh our sorrowful dying into holy, blissful life.

For I saw full surely that ever as our contrariness worketh to us here in earth pain, shame, and sorrow, right so, on the contrary wise, grace worketh to us in heaven solace, worship, and bliss; and overpassing. And so far forth, that when we come up and receive the sweet reward which grace hath wrought for us, then we shall thank and bless our Lord, endlessly rejoicing that ever we suffered woe. And that shall be for a property of blessed love that we shall know in God which we could never have known without woe going before.

And when I saw all this, it behoved me needs to grant that the mercy of God and the forgiveness is to slacken and waste *our* wrath.

CHAPTER XLIX

"Where our Lord appeareth, peace is taken, and wrath hath no place." "Immediately is the soul made at one with God when it is truly set at peace in itself"

For this was an high marvel to the soul which was continually shewed in all the Revelations, and was with great diligence beholden, that our Lord God, anent Himself may not forgive, for He may not be wroth: it were impossible. For this was shewed: that our life is all grounded and rooted in love, and without love we may not live; and therefore to the soul that of His special grace seeth so far into the high, marvellous Goodness of God, and seeth that we are endlessly oned to Him in love, it is the most impossible that may be, that God should be wroth. For wrath and friendship be two contraries. For He that wasteth and destroyeth our wrath and maketh us meek and mild,—it behoveth needs to be that He [Himself] be ever one in love, meek and mild: which is contrary to wrath.

For I saw full surely that where our Lord appeareth, peace is taken and wrath hath no place. For I saw no manner of wrath in God, neither for short time nor for long;—for in sooth, as to my sight, if God might be wroth for an instant, we should never have life nor place nor being. For as verily as we have our being of the endless Might of God and of the endless Wisdom and of the endless Goodness, so verily we have our keeping in the endless Might of God, in the endless Wisdom, and in the endless Goodness. For though we feel in ourselves, [frail] wretches, debates and strifes, yet are we all-mannerful enclosed in the mildness of God and in His meekness, in His benignity and in His graciousness. For I saw full surely that all our endless friendship, our place, our life and our being, is in God.

For that same endless Goodness that keepeth us when we sin, that we perish not, the same endless Goodness continually treateth in us a peace against our wrath and our contrarious falling, and maketh us to see our need with a true dread, and mightily to seek unto God to have forgiveness, with a gracious desire of our salvation. And though we, by the wrath and the contrariness that is in us, be now in tribulation, distress, and woe, as falleth to our blindness and frailty, yet are we *securely* safe by the merciful keeping of God, that we perish not. But we are not *blissfully* safe, in having of our endless joy, till we be all in peace and in love: that is to say, full pleased with God and with all His works, and with all His judgments, and loving and peaceable with our self and with our even-Christians and with all that God loveth, as love beseemeth. And this doeth God's Goodness in us.

Thus saw I that God is our very Peace, and He is our sure Keeper when we are ourselves in unpeace, and He continually worketh to bring us into endless peace. And thus when we, by the working of mercy and grace, be made meek and mild, we are fully safe; suddenly is the soul oned to God when it is truly peaced in itself: for in Him is found no wrath. And thus I saw when we are all in peace and in love, we find no contrariness, nor no manner of letting through that contrariness which is now in us; [nay], our Lord of His Goodness maketh it to us full profitable. For that contrariness is cause of our tribulations and all our woe, and our Lord Jesus taketh them and sendeth them up to Heaven, and there are they made more sweet and delectable than heart may think or tongue may tell. And when we come thither we shall find them ready, all turned into very fair and endless worships. Thus is God our steadfast Ground: and He shall be our full bliss and make us unchangeable, as He is, when we are there.

CHAPTER L

"The blame of our sin continually hangeth upon us." "In the sight of God the soul that shall be saved was never dead, nor ever shall be dead"

And in this life mercy and forgiveness is our way and evermore leadeth us to grace. And by the tempest and the sorrow that we fall into on our part, we be often dead as to man's doom in earth; but in the sight of God the soul that shall be saved was never dead, nor ever shall be.

But yet here I wondered and marvelled with all the diligence of my soul, saying thus within me: *Good Lord, I see Thee that art very Truth; and I know in truth that we sin grievously every day and be much blameworthy; and I may neither leave the knowing of Thy truth, nor do I see Thee shew to us any manner of blame. How may this be?*

For I knew by the common teaching of Holy Church and by mine own feeling, that the blame of our sin continually hangeth upon us, from the first man unto the time that we come up unto heaven: then was this my marvel that I saw our Lord God shewing to us no more blame than if we were as clean and as holy as Angels be in heaven. And between these two contraries my reason was greatly travailed through my blindness, and could have no rest for dread that His blessed presence should pass from my sight and I be left in unknowing [of] how He beholdeth us in our sin. For either [it] behoved me to see in God that sin was all done away, or else me behoved to see in God how He seeth it, whereby I might truly know how it belongeth to me to see sin, and the manner of our blame. My longing endured, Him continually beholding;—and yet I could have no patience for great straits and perplexity, thinking: *If I take it thus that we be no sinners and not blameworthy, it seemeth as I should err and fail of knowing of this truth; and if it be so that we be sinners and blameworthy,— Good Lord, how may it then be that I cannot see this true thing in Thee, which art my God, my Maker, in whom I desire to see all truths?*

For three points make me hardy to ask it. The first is, because it is so low a thing: for if it were an high thing I should be a-dread. The second is, that it is so common: for if it were special and privy, also I should be a-dread. The third is, that it needeth me to know it (as methinketh) if I shall live here for knowing of good and evil, whereby I may, by reason and grace, the more dispart them asunder, and love goodness and hate evil, as Holy Church teacheth. I cried inwardly, with all my might seeking unto God for help, saying thus: *Ah! Lord Jesus, King of bliss, how shall I be eased? Who shall teach me and tell me that [thing] me needeth to know, if I may not at this time see it in Thee?*

CHAPTER LI

"He is the Head, and we be His members." "Therefore our Father nor may nor will more blame assign to us than to His own Son, precious and worthy Christ"

And then our Courteous Lord answered in shewing full mistily a wonderful example of a Lord that hath a Servant: and He gave me sight to my understanding of both. Which sight was shewed doubly in the Lord and doubly in the Servant: the one part was shewed spiritually in bodily likeness, and the other part was shewed more spiritually, without bodily likeness.

For the first [sight], thus, I saw two persons in bodily likeness: that is to say, a Lord and a Servant; and therewith God gave me spiritual understanding. The Lord sitteth stately in rest and in peace; the Servant standeth by afore his Lord reverently, ready to do his Lord's will. The Lord looketh upon his Servant full lovingly and sweetly, and meekly he sendeth him to a certain place to do his will. The Servant not only he goeth, but suddenly he starteth, and runneth in great haste, for love to do his Lord's will. And anon he falleth into a slade, and taketh full great hurt. And then he groaneth and moaneth and waileth and struggleth, but he neither may rise nor help himself by no manner of way.

And of all this the most mischief that I saw him in, was failing of comfort: for he could not turn his face to look upon his loving Lord, which was to him full near,—in Whom is full comfort;—but as a man that was feeble and unwise for the time, he turned his mind to his feeling and endured in woe.

In which woe he suffered seven great pains. The first was the sore bruising that he took in his falling, which was to him feelable pain; the second was the heaviness of his body; the third was feebleness following from these two; the fourth, that he was blinded in his reason and stunned in his mind, so far forth that almost he had forgotten his own love; the fifth was that he might not rise; the sixth was most marvellous to me, and that was that he lay all alone: I looked all about and beheld, and far nor near, high nor low, I saw to him no help; the seventh was that the place which he lay on was a long, hard, and grievous [place].

I marvelled how this Servant might meekly suffer there all this woe, and I beheld with carefulness to learn if I could perceive in him any fault, or if the Lord should assign to him any blame. And in sooth there was none seen: for only his goodwill and his great desire was cause of his falling; and he was unlothful, and as good inwardly as when he stood afore his Lord, ready to do his will. And right thus continually his loving Lord full tenderly beholdeth him. But now with a *double* manner of Regard: one outward, full meekly and mildly, with great ruth and pity,—and this was of the first [sight], another *inward,* more spiritually,—and this was shewed with a leading of mine understanding into the Lord, [in the] which I saw Him highly rejoicing for the worshipful restoring that He will and shall bring His Servant to by His plenteous grace; and this was of that other shewing.

And now [was] my understanding led again into the first [sight]; both keeping in mind. Then saith this courteous Lord in his meaning: *Lo, lo, my loved Servant, what harm and distress he hath taken in my service for my love,—yea, and for his goodwill. Is it not fitting that I award him [for] his affright and his dread, his hurt and his maim and all his woe? And not only this, but falleth it not to me to give a gift that [shall] be better to him, and more worshipful, than his own wholeness should have been?—or else methinketh I should do him no grace.*

And in this an inward spiritual Shewing of the Lord's meaning descended into my soul: in which I saw that it behoveth needs to be, by virtue of His great [Goodness] and His own worship, that His dearworthy Servant, which He loved so much, should be verily and blissfully rewarded, above that he should have been if he had not fallen. Yea, and so far forth, that his falling and his woe, that he hath taken thereby, shall be turned into high and overpassing worship and endless bliss.

And at this point the shewing of the example vanished, and our good Lord led forth mine understanding in sight and in shewing of the Revelation to the end. But notwithstanding all this forth-leading, the marvelling over the example went never from me: for methought it was given me for an answer to my desire, and yet could I not take therein full understanding to mine ease at that time. For in the Servant that was shewed for Adam, as I shall tell, I saw many diverse properties that might in no manner of way be assigned to single Adam. And thus in that time I stood for much part in unknowing: for the full understanding of this marvellous example was not given me in that time. In which mighty example three properties of the Revelation be yet greatly hid; and notwithstanding this [further forthleading], I saw and understood that every Shewing is full of secret things [left hid].

And therefore me behoveth now to tell three properties in which I am somewhat eased. The first is the beginning of teaching that I understood therein, in the same time; the second is the inward teaching that I have understood therein afterward; the third, all the whole Revelation from the beginning to the end (that is to say of this Book) which our Lord God of His goodness bringeth oftentimes freely to the sight of mine understanding. And these three are so oned, as to my understanding, that I cannot, nor may, dispart them. And by these three, as one, I have teaching whereby I ought to believe and trust in our Lord God, that of the same goodness of which He shewed it, and for the same end, right so, of the same goodness and for the same end He shall declare it to us when it is His will.

For, twenty years after the time of the Shewing, save three months, I had teaching inwardly, as I shall tell: *It belongeth to thee to take heed to all the properties and conditions that were shewed in the example, though thou think that they be misty and indifferent to thy sight.* I assented willingly, with great desire, and inwardly [beheld] with heedfulness all the points and properties that were shewed in the same time, as far forth as my wits and understanding would serve: beginning my beholding at the Lord and at the Servant, and the manner of sitting of the Lord, and the place that he sat on, and the colour of his clothing and the manner of shape, and his countenance without, and his nobleness and his goodness within; at the manner of standing of the Servant, and the place where, and how; at his manner of clothing, the colour and the shape; at his outward having and at his inward goodness and his unloathfulness.

The Lord that sat stately in rest and in peace, I understood that He is God. The Servant that stood afore the Lord, I understood that it was shewed for Adam: that is to say, one man was shewed, that time, and his falling, to make it thereby understood how God beholdeth All-Man and his falling. For in the sight of God all man is one man, and one man is all man. This man was hurt in his might and made full feeble; and he was stunned in his understanding so that he [was] turned from the beholding of his Lord. But his will was kept whole in God's sight;—for his will I saw our Lord commend and approve. But himself was letted and blinded from the knowing of this will; and this is to him great sorrow and grievous distress: for neither doth he see clearly his loving Lord, which is to him full meek and mild, nor doth he see truly what himself is in the sight of his loving Lord. And well I wot when these two are wisely and truly seen, we shall get rest and peace here in part, and the fulness of the bliss of Heaven, by His plenteous grace.

And this was a beginning of teaching which I saw in the same time, whereby I might come to know in what manner He beholdeth us in our sin. And then I saw that only Pain blameth and punisheth, and our courteous Lord comforteth and sorroweth; and ever He is to the soul in glad Cheer, loving, and longing to bring us to His bliss.

The place that the Lord sat on was simple, on the earth, barren and desert, alone in wilderness; his clothing was ample and full seemly, as falleth to a Lord; the colour of his cloth was blue as azure, most sad and fair, his cheer was merciful; the colour of his face was fair-brown,—with full seemly features; his eyes were black, most fair and seemly, shewing [*outward*] full of lovely *pity*, and [shewing], *within* him, an high Regard, long and broad, all full of endless heavens. And the lovely looking wherewith He looked upon His Servant continually,—and especially in his falling,—methought it might melt our hearts for love and burst them in two for joy. The fair looking shewed [itself] of a seemly mingledness which was marvellous to behold: the one [part] was Ruth and Pity, the other was Joy and Bliss. The Joy and Bliss passeth as far Ruth and Pity as Heaven is above earth: the Pity was earthly and the Bliss was heavenly: the Ruth and Pity of the Father was [in regard] of the falling of Adam, which is His most loved creature; the Joy and Bliss was [in regard] of His dearworthy Son, which is even with the Father. The Merciful Beholding of His Countenance of love fulfilled all earth and descended down with Adam into hell, with which continuant pity

Adam was kept from endless death. And thus Mercy and Pity dwelleth with mankind unto the time we come up into Heaven.

But man is blinded in this life and therefore we may not see our Father, God, as He is. And what time that He of His goodness willeth to shew Himself to man, He sheweth Himself homely, as man. Notwithstanding, I reason, in verity we ought to know and believe that the Father is not man.

But his sitting on the earth barren and desert, is to signify this:—He made man's soul to be His own City and His dwelling-place: which is most pleasing to Him of all His works. And what time that man was fallen into sorrow and pain, he was not all seemly to serve in that noble office; and therefore our Lord Father would prepare Himself no other place, but would sit upon the earth abiding mankind, which is mingled with earth, till what time by His grace His dearworthy Son had brought again His City into the noble fairness with His hard travail. The blueness of the clothing betokeneth His steadfastness; the brownness of his fair face, with the seemly blackness of the eyes, was most accordant to shew His holy soberness. The length and breadth of his garments, which were fair, flaming about, betokeneth that He hath, beclosed in Him, all Heavens, and all Joy and Bliss: and this was shewed in a touch [of time], where I have said: *Mine understanding was led into the Lord*; in which [inward shewing] I saw Him highly *rejoice* for the worshipful restoring that He will and shall bring His servant to by His plenteous grace.

And yet I marvelled, beholding the Lord and the Servant aforesaid. I saw the Lord sit stately, and the Servant standing reverently afore his Lord. In which Servant there is double understanding, one *without*, another *within. Outwardly*:—he was clad simply, as a labourer which were got ready for his toil; and he stood full near the Lord—not evenly in front of him, but in part to one side, on the left. His clothing was a white kirtle, single, old, and all defaced, dyed with sweat of his body, strait-fitting to him, and short—as it were an handful beneath the knee; [thread]bare, seeming as it should soon be worn out, ready to be ragged and rent. And of this I marvelled greatly, thinking: this is now an unseemly clothing for the Servant that is so greatly loved to stand in afore so worshipful a Lord. And *inwardly* in him was shewed a ground of love: which love that he had to the Lord was even-like to the love that the Lord had to him.

The wisdom of the Servant saw inwardly that there was one thing to do which should be to the worship of the Lord. And the Servant, for love, having no regard to himself nor to nothing that might befall him, hastily he started and ran at the sending of his Lord, to do that thing which was his will and his worship. For it seemed by his outward clothing as he had been a continuant labourer of long time, and by the *inward sight* that I had both of the Lord and the Servant it seemed that he was a new [one], that is to say, new beginning to travail: which Servant was never sent out afore.

There was a treasure in the earth which the Lord loved. I marvelled and thought what it might be, and I was answered in mine understanding: *It is a food which is delectable and pleasant to the Lord.* For I saw the Lord sit as a man, and I saw neither meat nor drink wherewith to serve him. This was one marvel. Another marvel was that this majestic Lord had no servant but one, and him he sent out. I beheld, thinking what manner of labour it might be that the Servant should do. And then I understood that he should do the greatest labour and hardest travail: that is, he should be a gardener, delve and dyke, toil and sweat, and turn the earth upside-down, and seek the deepness, and water the plants in time. And in this he should continue his travail and make sweet floods to run, and noble and plenteous fruits to spring, which he should bring afore the Lord to serve him therewith to his desire. And he should never turn again till he had prepared this food all ready as he knew that it pleased the Lord. And then he should take this food, with the drink in the food, and bear it full worshipfully afore the Lord. And all this time the Lord should sit in the same place, abiding his Servant whom he sent out.

And yet I marvelled from whence the Servant came. For I saw in the Lord that HE hath within Himself endless life, and all manner of goodness, save that treasure that was in the earth. And [also] *that* [treasure] was grounded in the Lord in marvellous deepness of endless love, but it was not all to His worship till the Servant had thus nobly prepared it, and brought it before Him in himself present. And without the Lord was nothing but wilderness. And I understood not all what this example meant, and therefore I marvelled whence the Servant came.

In the Servant is comprehended the Second Person in the Trinity; and in the Servant is comprehended Adam: that is to say, All-Man. And therefore when I say the *Son*, it meaneth the Godhead which is even with the Father; and when I say the *Servant*, it meaneth Christ's Manhood, which is rightful Adam. By the nearness of the Servant is understood the Son, and by the standing on the left side is understood Adam. The Lord is the Father, God; the Servant is the Son, Christ Jesus; the Holy Ghost is Even Love which is in them both.

When Adam fell, God's Son fell: because of the rightful oneing which had been made in heaven, God's Son might not [be disparted] from Adam. (For by Adam I understand All-Man.) Adam fell from life to death, into the deep of this wretched world, and after that into hell: God's Son fell with Adam, into the deep of the Maiden's womb, who was the fairest daughter of Adam; and for this end: to excuse Adam from blame in heaven and in earth; and mightily He fetched him out of hell.

By the wisdom and goodness that was in the Servant is understood God's Son; by the poor clothing as a labourer standing near the left side, is understood the Manhood and Adam, with all the scathe and feebleness that followeth. For in all this our good Lord shewed His own Son and Adam but *one* Man. The virtue and the goodness that we have is of Jesus Christ, the feebleness and the blindness that we have is of Adam: which two were shewed in the Servant.

And thus hath our good Lord Jesus taken upon Him all our blame, and therefore our Father nor may nor will more blame assign to us than to His own Son, dearworthy Christ. Thus was He, the Servant, afore His coming into earth standing ready afore the Father in purpose, till what time He would send Him to do that worshipful deed by which mankind was brought again into heaven;—that is to say, notwithstanding that He is God, even with the Father as anent the Godhead. But in His foreseeing purpose that He would be Man, to save man in fulfilling of His Father's will, so He stood afore His Father as a Servant, willingly taking upon Him all our charge. And then He started full readily at the Father's will, and anon He fell full low, into the Maiden's womb, having no regard to Himself nor to His hard pains.

The white kirtle is the flesh; the singleness is that there was right nought atwix the Godhead and Manhood; the straitness is poverty; the eld is of Adam's wearing; the defacing, of sweat of Adam's travail; the shortness sheweth the Servant's labour.

And thus I saw the Son saying in His meaning: *Lo! my dear Father, I stand before Thee in Adam's kirtle, all ready to start and to run: I would be in the earth to do Thy worship when it is Thy will to send me. How long shall I desire?* Full soothfastly wist the Son when it would be the Father's will and how long He should desire: that is to say, [He wist it] anent the Godhead: for He is the Wisdom of the Father; wherefore this question was shewed with understanding of the *Manhood* of Christ. For all mankind that shall be saved by the sweet Incarnation and blissful Passion of Christ, all is the Manhood of Christ: for He is the Head and we be His members. To which members the day and the time is unknown when every passing woe and sorrow shall have an end, and the everlasting joy and bliss shall be fulfilled; which day and time for to see, all the Company of Heaven longeth. And all that shall be under heaven that shall come thither, their way is by longing and desire. Which desire and longing was shewed in the Servant's standing afore the Lord,—or else thus in the Son's standing afore the Father in Adam's kirtle. For the longing and desire of all Mankind that shall be saved appeared in Jesus: for Jesus is All that shall be saved, and All that shall be saved is Jesus. And all of the Charity of God; with obedience, meekness, and patience, and virtues that belong to us.

Also in this marvellous example I have teaching with me as it were the beginning of an A.B.C., whereby I have some understanding of our Lord's meaning. For the secret things of the Revelation be hid therein;—notwithstanding that *all* the Shewings are full of secret things. The *sitting* of the Father betokeneth His Godhead: that is to say, by shewing of rest and peace: for in the Godhead may be no travail. And that He shewed Himself as *Lord*, betokeneth His [governance] to our manhood. The *standing* of the Servant betokeneth travail; *on one side*, and on the *left*, betokeneth that he was not all worthy to stand even-right afore the Lord; his *starting* was the Godhead, and the *running* was the Manhood: for the Godhead started from the Father into the Maiden's womb, falling into the taking of our Kind. And in this falling he took great sore: the *sore* that He took was our flesh, in which He had also swiftly feeling of deadly pains. That he stood *adread* before the Lord and not even-right, betokeneth that His clothing was not seemly to stand in even-right afore the Lord, nor *that* might not, nor should not, be His office while He was a labourer; nor also He might not sit in rest and peace with the Lord till He had won His peace rightfully with His hard travail; and that he stood by the *left* side [betokeneth] that the Father left His own Son, willingly, in the Manhood to suffer all man's pains, without sparing of Him. By that *his kirtle was in point to be ragged and rent*, is understood the blows, the scourgings, the thorns and the nails, the drawing and the dragging, His tender flesh rending. (As I saw in some part [before] how the flesh was rent from the skull, falling in pieces until the time when the bleeding ceased, and then it began to dry again, cleaving to the bone.) And by the *struggling and writhing, groaning and moaning,* is understood that He might never rise almightily from the time that He was fallen into the Maiden's womb, till his body was slain and dead, He yielding the soul into the Father's hands with all Mankind for whom He was sent.

And at this point He began first to shew His might: for He went into Hell, and when He was there He raised up the great Root out of the deep deepness which rightfully was knit to Him in high Heaven. The body was in the grave till Easter-morrow, and from that time He lay nevermore. For then was rightfully ended the struggling and the writhing, the groaning and the moaning. And our foul deadly flesh that God's Son took on Him, which was Adam's old kirtle, strait, [worn]-bare, and short, was then by our Saviour made fair, new, white and bright and of endless cleanness; loose and long; fairer and richer than was then the clothing which [before] I saw on the Father: for that clothing was blue, but Christ's clothing is [coloured] now of a fair seemly medlour, which is so marvellous that I can it not describe: for it is all of very worships.

Now sitteth not the Son on earth in wilderness, but He sitteth in His noblest Seat, which He made in Heaven most to His pleasing. Now standeth not the Son afore the Father as a Servant afore the Lord dreadingly, meanly clad, in part naked; but He standeth afore the Father even-right, richly clad in blissful largeness, with a Crown upon His head of precious richness. For it was shewed that *we be His Crown*: which Crown is the Joy of the Father, the Worship of the Son, the Satisfying of the Holy Ghost, and endless marvellous Bliss to all that be in Heaven. Now standeth not the Son afore the Father on the left side, as a labourer, but He sitteth on His Father's right hand, in endless rest and peace. (But it is not meant that the Son sitteth on the right hand, side by side, as one man sitteth by another in this life,—for there is no such sitting, as to my sight, in the Trinity,—but He sitteth on His Father's right hand,—that is to say: in the highest nobleness of the Father's joys.) Now is the Spouse, God's Son, in peace with His loved Wife, which is the Fair Maiden of endless Joy.

Now sitteth the Son, Very God and Man, in His City in rest and peace: which [City] His Father hath adight to Him of His endless purpose; and the Father in the Son; and the Holy Ghost in the Father and in the Son.

CHAPTER LII

"We have now matter of mourning: for our sin is cause of Christ's pains; and we have, lastingly, matter of joy: for endless love made Him to suffer"

And thus I saw that God rejoiceth that He is our Father, and God rejoiceth that He is our Mother, and God rejoiceth that He is our Very Spouse and our soul is His loved Wife. And Christ rejoiceth that He is our Brother, and Jesus rejoiceth that He is our Saviour. These are five high joys, as I understand, in which He willeth that we enjoy; Him praising, Him thanking, Him loving, Him endlessly blessing.

All that shall be saved, we have in us, for the time of this life, a marvellous mingling both of weal and woe: we have in us our Lord Jesus uprisen, we have in us the wretchedness and the mischief of Adam's falling, dying. By Christ we are steadfastly kept, and by His grace touching us we are raised into sure trust of salvation. And by Adam's falling we are so broken, in our feeling, in diverse manners by sins and by sundry pains, in which we are made dark, that scarsely we can take any comfort. But in our intent we abide in God, and faithfully trust to have mercy and grace; and this is His own working in us. And of His goodness He openeth the eye of our understanding, by which we have sight, sometime more and sometime less, according as God giveth ability to receive. And now we are raised into the one, and now we are suffered to fall into the other.

And thus is this medley so marvellous in us that scarsely we know of our self or of our even-Christian in what way we stand, for the marvellousness of this sundry feeling. But that same Holy Assent, *that* we assent to God when we feel Him, truly setting our will to be with Him, with all our heart, and with all our soul, and with all our might. And then we hate and despise our evil stirrings and all that might be occasion of sin, spiritual and bodily. And yet nevertheless when this sweetness is hid, we fall again into blindness, and so into woe and tribulation in diverse manners. But then is this our comfort, that we *know in our faith* that by virtue of Christ which is our Keeper, we assent never thereto, but we groan there-against, and dure on, in pain and woe, praying, unto that time that He sheweth Him again to us.

And thus we stand in this medley all the days of our life. But He willeth that we trust that He is lastingly with as. And that in three manner.— He is with us in Heaven, very Man, in His own Person, us updrawing; and that was shewed in [the Shewing of] the Spiritual Thirst. And He is with us in earth, us leading; and that was shewed in the Third [Shewing], where I saw God in a Point. And He is with us in our soul, endlessly dwelling, us ruling and keeping; and that was shewed in the Sixteenth [Shewing], as I shall tell.

And thus in the Servant was shewed the scathe and blindness of Adam's falling; and in the Servant was shewed the wisdom and goodness of God's Son. And in the Lord was shewed the ruth and pity of Adam's woe, and in the Lord was shewed the high nobility and the endless worship that Mankind is come to by the virtue of the Passion and death of His dearworthy Son. And therefore mightily He joyeth in his falling for the high raising and fulness of bliss that Mankind is come to, overpassing that we should have had if he had not fallen.— And thus to see this overpassing nobleness was mine understanding led into God in the same time that I saw the Servant fall.

And thus we have, now, matter of mourning: for our sin is cause of Christ's pains; and we have, lastingly, matter of joy: for endless love made Him to suffer. And therefore the creature that seeth and feeleth the working of love by grace, hateth nought but sin: for of all things, to my sight, love and hate are [the] hardest and most unmeasureable contraries. And notwithstanding all this, I saw and understood in our Lord's meaning that we may not in this life keep us from sin as wholly in full cleanness as we shall be in Heaven. But we may well by grace keep us from the sins which would lead us to endless pains, as Holy Church teacheth us; and eschew venial [ones] reasonably up to our might. And if we by our blindness and our wretchedness any time fall, we should readily rise, knowing the sweet touching of grace, and with all our will amend us upon the teaching of Holy Church, according as the sin is grievous, and go forthwith to God in love; and neither, on the one side, fall over low, inclining to despair, nor, on the other side, be over-reckless, as if we made no matter of it; but nakedly acknowledge our feebleness, finding that we may not stand a twinkling of an eye but by Keeping of grace, and reverently cleave to God, on Him only trusting.

For after one wise is the Beholding by God, and after another wise is the Beholding by man. For it belongeth to man meekly to accuse himself, and it belongeth to the proper Goodness of our Lord God courteously to excuse man. And these be two parts that were shewed in the double Manner of Regard with which the Lord beheld the falling of His loved Servant. The one was shewed outward, very meekly and mildly, with great ruth and pity; and that of endless Love. And right thus willeth our Lord that we accuse our self, earnestly and truly seeing and knowing our falling and all the harms that come thereof; seeing and learning that we can never restore it; and therewith that we earnestly and truly see and know His everlasting love that He hath to us, and His plenteous mercy. And thus graciously to see and know both together is the meek accusing that our Lord asketh of us, and Himself worketh it where it is. And this is the lower part of man's life, and it was shewed in the [Lord's] *outward* manner of Regard. In which shewing I saw *two* parts: the one is the rueful falling of man, the other is the worshipful Satisfaction that our Lord hath made for man.

The other manner of Regard was shewed *inward*: and that was more highly and all [fully] *one*. For the life and the virtue that we have in the lower part is of the higher, and it cometh down to us [from out] of the Natural love of the [high] Self, by [the working of] grace. Atwix [the life of] the one and [the life of] the other there is right nought: for it is all one love. Which one blessed love hath now, in us, double working: for in the lower part are pains and passions, mercies and forgiveness, and such other that are profitable; but in the higher part are none of these, but all one high love and marvellous joy: in which joy all pains are highly restored. And in this [time] our Lord showed not only our Excusing [from blame, in His beholding of our higher part], but the worshipful nobility that He shall bring us to [by the working of grace in our lower part], turning all our blame [that is therein, from our falling] into endless worship [when we be oned to the high Self above].

CHAPTER LIII

"In every soul that shall be saved is a Godly Will that never assented to sin, nor ever shall." "Ere that He made us He loved us, and when we were made we loved Him"

And I saw that He willeth that we understand He taketh not harder the falling of any creature that shall be saved than He took the falling of Adam, which, we know, was endlessly loved and securely kept in the time of all his need, and now is blissfully restored in high overpassing joy. For our Lord is so good, so gentle, and so courteous, that He may never assign default [in those] in whom He shall ever be blessed and praised.

And in this that I have now told was my desire in part answered, and my great difficulty some deal eased, by the lovely, gracious Shewing of our good Lord. In which Shewing I saw and understood full surely that in every soul that shall be saved is a Godly Will that never assented to sin, nor ever shall: which Will is so good that it may never will evil, but evermore continually it willeth good; and worketh good in the sight of God. Therefore our Lord willeth that we know this in the Faith and the belief; and especially that we have all this blessed Will whole and safe in our Lord Jesus Christ. For that same Kind that Heaven shall be filled with behoveth needs, of God's rightfulness, so to have been knit and oned to Him, that therein was kept a Substance which might never, nor should, be parted from Him; and *that* through His own Good Will in His endless foreseeing purpose.

But notwithstanding this rightful knitting and this endless oneing, yet the redemption and the again-buying of mankind is needful and speedful in everything, as it is done for the same intent and to the same end that Holy Church in our Faith us teacheth.

For I saw that God *began* never to love mankind: for right the same that mankind shall be in endless bliss, fulfilling the joy of God as anent His works, right so the same, mankind hath been in the foresight of God: known and loved from without beginning in his rightful intent. By the endless assent of the full accord of all the Trinity, the Mid-Person willed to be Ground and Head of this fair Kind: out of Whom we be all come, in Whom we be all enclosed, into Whom we shall all wend, in Him finding our full Heaven in everlasting joy, by the foreseeing purpose of all the blessed Trinity from without beginning.

For ere that He made us He loved us, and when we were made we loved Him. And this is a Love that is *made*, [to our Kindly Substance], [by virtue] of the Kindly Substantial *Goodness* of the Holy Ghost; Mighty, in Reason, [by virtue] of the *Might* of the Father; and Wise, in Mind, [by virtue] of the *Wisdom* of the Son. And thus is Man's Soul made by God and in the same point knit to God.

And thus I understand that man's Soul is made of nought: that is to say, it is made, but of nought that is made. And thus:—When God should make man's body He took the clay of earth, which is a matter mingled and gathered of all bodily things; and thereof He made man's body. But to the making of man's Soul He would take right nought, but made it. And thus is the Nature-made rightfully oned to the Maker, which is Substantial Nature not-made: that is, God. And therefore it is that there may nor shall be right nought atwix God and man's Soul.

And in this endless Love man's Soul is kept whole, as the matter of the Revelations signifieth and sheweth: in which endless Love we be led and kept of God and never shall be lost. For He willeth we be aware that our Soul is a life, which life of His Goodness and His Grace shall last in Heaven without end, Him loving, Him thanking, Him praising. And right the same that we shall be without end, the same we were treasured in God and hid, known and loved from without beginning.

Wherefore He would have us understand that the noblest thing that ever He made is mankind: and the fullest Substance and the highest Virtue is the blessed Soul of Christ. And furthermore He would have us understand that His dear worthy Soul [of Manhood] was preciously knit to Him in the making [by Him of Manhood's Substantial Nature] which knot is so subtle and so mighty that (it)—[man's soul]—is oned into God: in which oneing it is made endlessly holy. Furthermore He would have us know that all the souls that shall be saved in Heaven without end, are knit and oned in this oneing and made holy in this holiness.

CHAPTER LIV

"Faith is nought else but a right understanding, with true belief and
sure trust, of our Being: that we are in God, and God is in us: Whom
we see not"

And because of this great, endless love that God hath to all Mankind,
He maketh no disparting in love between the blessed Soul of Christ
and the least soul that shall be saved. For it is full easy to believe and
to trust that the dwelling of the blessed Soul of Christ is full high in
the glorious Godhead, and verily, as I understand in our Lord's
signifying, where the blessed Soul of Christ is, there is the Substance
of all the souls that shall be saved by Christ.

Highly ought we to rejoice that God dwelleth in our soul, and much
more highly ought we to rejoice that our soul dwelleth in God. Our
soul is *made* to be God's dwelling-place; and the dwelling-place of the
soul is God, Which is *unmade*. And high understanding it is, inwardly
to see and know that God, which is our Maker, dwelleth in our soul;
and an higher understanding it is, inwardly to see and to know that
our soul, that is made, dwelleth in God's Substance: of which
Substance, God, we are that we are.

And I saw no difference between God and our Substance: but as it
were all God; and yet mine understanding took that our Substance is
in God: that is to say, that God is God, and our Substance is a creature
in God. For the Almighty Truth of the Trinity is our Father: for He
made us and keepeth us in Him; and the deep Wisdom of the Trinity
is our Mother, in Whom we are all enclosed; the high Goodness of the
Trinity is our Lord, and in Him we are enclosed, and He in us. We are
enclosed in the Father, and we are enclosed in the Son, and we are
enclosed in the Holy Ghost. And the Father is enclosed in us, and the
Son is enclosed in us, and the Holy Ghost is enclosed in us:
Almightiness, All-Wisdom, All-Goodness: one God, one Lord.

And our faith is a Virtue that cometh of our Nature-Substance into
our Sense-soul by the Holy Ghost; in which all our virtues come to us:
for without that, no man may receive virtue. For it is nought else but
a right understanding, with true belief, and sure trust, of our Being:
that we are in God, and God in us, Whom we see not. And this virtue,
with all other that God hath ordained to us coming therein, worketh

in us great things. For Christ's merciful working is in us, and we graciously accord to Him through the gifts and the virtues of the Holy Ghost. This working maketh that we are Christ's children, and Christian in living.

CHAPTER LV

"Christ is our Way"—"Mankind shall be restored from double death"

And thus Christ is our Way, us surely leading in His laws, and Christ in His body mightily beareth us up into heaven. For I saw that Christ, us all having in Him that shall be saved by Him, worshipfully presenteth His Father in heaven with us; which present full thankfully His Father receiveth, and courteously giveth it to His Son, Jesus Christ: which gift and working is joy to the Father, and bliss to the Son, and pleasing to the Holy Ghost. And of all things that belong to us [to do], it is most pleasing to our Lord that we enjoy in this joy which is in the blessed Trinity [in virtue] of our salvation. (And this was seen in the Ninth Shewing, where it speaketh more of this matter.) And notwithstanding all our feeling of woe or weal, God willeth that we should understand and hold by faith that we are more verily in heaven than in earth.

Our Faith cometh of the natural Love of our soul, and of the clear light of our Reason, and of the steadfast Mind which we have from God in our first making. And what time that our soul is inspired into our body, in which we are made sensual, so soon mercy and grace begin to work, having of us care and keeping with pity and love: in which working the Holy Ghost formeth, in our Faith, *Hope* that we shall come again up above to our Substance, into the Virtue of Christ, increased and fulfilled through the Holy Ghost. Thus I understood that the sense-soul is grounded in Nature, in Mercy, and in Grace: which Ground enableth us to receive gifts that lead us to endless life.

For I saw full assuredly that our Substance is in God, and also I saw that in our sense-soul God is: for in the self-[same] point that our Soul is made sensual, in the self-[same] point is the City of God ordained to Him from without beginning; into which seat He cometh, and never shall remove [from] it. For God is never out of the soul: in which He dwelleth blissfully without end. And this was seen in the Sixteenth Shewing where it saith: *The place that Jesus taketh in our soul, He shall never remove [from] it.* And all the gifts that God may give to creatures, He hath given to His Son Jesus for us: which gifts He, dwelling in us, hath enclosed in Him unto the time that we be waxen and grown,—our soul with our body and our body with our soul, either of them taking help of other,—till we be brought up unto stature, as nature worketh. And then, in the ground of nature, with working of mercy, the Holy Ghost graciously inspireth into us gifts leading to endless life.

And thus was my understanding led of God to see in Him and to understand, to perceive and to know, that our soul is *made-trinity*, like to the unmade blissful Trinity, known and loved from without beginning, and in the making oned to the Maker, as it is aforesaid. This sight was full sweet and marvellous to behold, peaceable, restful, sure, and delectable.

And because of the worshipful oneing that was thus made by God betwixt the soul and body, it behoveth needs to be that mankind shall be restored from double death: which restoring might never be until the time that the Second Person in the Trinity had taken the lower part of man's nature; to Whom the highest [part] was oned in the First-making. And these two parts were in Christ, the higher and the lower: which is but one Soul; the higher part was one in peace with God, in full joy and bliss; the lower part, which is sense-nature, suffered for the salvation of mankind.

And these two parts [in Christ] were seen and felt in the Eighth Shewing, in which my body was fulfilled with feeling and mind of Christ's Passion and His death, and furthermore with this was a subtile feeling and privy inward sight of the High Part which I was shewed in the same time when I could not, [even] for the friendly proffer [made to me], look up into Heaven: and that was because of that mighty beholding [that I had] of the Inward Life. Which Inward Life is that High Substance, that precious Soul, [of Christ], which is endlessly rejoicing in the Godhead.

CHAPTER LVI

"God is nearer to us than our own soul"
"We can never come to full knowing of God till we know first clearly
our own Soul"

And thus I saw full surely that it is readier to us to come to the knowing of God than to know our own Soul. For our Soul is so deep-grounded in God, and so endlessly treasured, that we may not come to the knowing thereof till we have first knowing of God, which is the Maker, to whom it is oned. But, notwithstanding, I saw that we have, for fulness, to desire wisely and truly to know our own Soul: whereby we are learned to seek it where it is, and that is, in God. And thus by gracious leading of the Holy Ghost, we should know them both in one: whether we be stirred to know God or our Soul, both [these stirrings] are good and true.

God is nearer to us than our own Soul: for He is [the] Ground in whom our Soul standeth, and He is [the] Mean that keepeth the Substance and the Sense-nature together so that they shall never dispart. For our soul sitteth in God in very rest, and our soul standeth in God in very strength, and our Soul is kindly rooted in God in endless love: and therefore if we will have knowledge of our Soul, and communing and dalliance therewith, it behoveth to seek unto our Lord God in whom it is enclosed. (And of this enclosement I saw and understood more in the Sixteenth Shewing, as I shall tell.)

And as anent our Substance and our Sense-part, both together may rightly be called our Soul: and that is because of the oneing that they have in God. The worshipful City that our Lord Jesus sitteth in is our Sense-soul, in which He is enclosed: and our Kindly Substance is enclosed in Jesus with the blessed Soul of Christ sitting in rest in the Godhead.

And I saw full surely that it behoveth needs to be that we should be in longing and in penance unto the time that we be led so deep into God that we verily and truly know our own Soul. And truly I saw that into this high deepness our good Lord Himself leadeth us in the same love that He made us, and in the same love that He bought us by Mercy and Grace through virtue of His blessed Passion. And notwithstanding all this, we may never come to full knowing of God till we know first clearly our own Soul. For until the time that our Soul is in its full powers we cannot be all fully holy: and that is [until the time] that our Sense-soul by the virtue of Christ's Passion be brought up to the Substance, with all the profits of our tribulation that our Lord shall make us to get by Mercy and Grace.

I had, in part, [experience of the] Touching [of God in the soul], and it is grounded in Nature. That is to say, our Reason is grounded in God, which is Substantial Naturehood. [Out] of this Substantial Naturehood Mercy and Grace springeth and spreadeth into us, working all things in fulfilling of our joy: these are our Ground in which we have our Increase and our Fulfilling.

These be three properties in one Goodness: and where one worketh, all work in the things which be *now* belonging to us. God willeth that we understand [this], desiring with all our heart to have knowing of them more and more unto the time that we be fulfilled: for fully to know them is nought else but endless joy and bliss that we shall have in Heaven, which God willeth should be begun here in knowing of His love.

For only by our Reason we may not profit, but if we have evenly therewith Mind and Love: nor only in our Nature-Ground that we have in God we may not be saved but if we have, coming of the same Ground, Mercy and Grace. For of these three working all together we receive all our Goodness. Of the which the first [gifts] are goods of Nature: for in our First making God gave us as full goods as we might receive in our spirit alone,—and also greater goods; but His foreseeing purpose in His endless wisdom willed that we should be double.

CHAPTER LVII

"In Christ our two natures are united"

And anent our Substance He made us noble, and so rich that evermore we work His will and His worship. (Where I say "we," it meaneth Man that shall be saved.) For soothly I saw that we are that which He loveth, and do that which Him pleaseth, lastingly without any stinting: and [that by virtue] of the great riches and of the high noble virtues by measure come to our soul what time it is knit to our body: in which knitting we are made Sensual.

And thus in our Substance we are full, and in our Sense-soul we fail: which failing God will restore and fulfil by working of Mercy and Grace plenteously flowing into us out of His own Nature-Goodness. And thus His Nature-Goodness maketh that Mercy and Grace work in us, and the Nature-goodness that we have of Him enableth us to receive the working of Mercy and Grace.

I saw that our nature is in God whole: in which [whole nature of Manhood] He maketh diversities flowing out of Him to work His will: whom Nature keepeth, and Mercy and Grace restoreth and fulfilleth. And of these none shall perish: for our nature that is the higher part is knit to God, in the making; and God is knit to our nature that is the lower part, in our flesh-taking: and thus in Christ our two natures are oned. For the Trinity is comprehended in Christ, in whom our higher part is grounded and rooted; and our lower part the Second Person hath taken: which nature first to Him was made-ready. For I saw full surely that all the works that God hath done, or ever shall, were fully known to Him and aforeseen from without beginning. And for Love He made Mankind, and for the same Love would be Man.

The next Good that we receive is our Faith, in which our profiting beginneth. And it cometh [out] of the high riches of our nature-Substance into our Sensual soul, and it is grounded in us through the Nature-Goodness of God, by the working of Mercy and Grace. And thereof come all other goods by which we are led and saved. For the Commandments of God come therein: in which we ought to have two manners of understanding: [the one is that we ought to understand and know] which are His biddings, to love and to keep them; the other is that we ought to know His forbiddings, to hate and to refuse them. For in these two is all our working comprehended. Also in our faith come the Seven Sacraments, each following other in order as God hath ordained them to us: and all manner of virtues.

For the same virtues that we have received of our Substance, given to us in Nature by the Goodness of God,—the same virtues by the working of Mercy are given to us in Grace through the Holy Ghost, *renewed*: which virtues and gifts are treasured to us in Jesus Christ. For in that same time that God knitted Himself to our body in the Virgin's womb, He took our Sensual soul: in which taking He, us all having enclosed in Him, oned it to our Substance: in which oneing He was perfect Man. For Christ having knit in Him each man that shall be saved, is perfect Man. Thus our Lady is our Mother in whom we are all enclosed and of her born, in Christ: (for she that is Mother of our Saviour is Mother of all that shall be saved in our Saviour;) and our Saviour is our Very Mother in whom we be endlessly borne, and never shall come out of Him.

Plenteously and fully and sweetly was this shewed, and it is spoken of in the First, where it saith: *We are all in Him enclosed and He is enclosed in us.* And that [enclosing of Him in us] is spoken of in the Sixteenth Shewing, where it saith: *He sitteth in our soul.*

For it is His good-pleasure to reign in our Understanding blissfully, and sit in our Soul restfully, and to dwell in our Soul endlessly, us all working into Him: in which working He willeth that we be His helpers, giving to Him all our attending, learning His lores, keeping His laws, desiring that all be done that He doeth; truly trusting in Him.

For soothly I saw that our Substance is in God.

CHAPTER LVIII

"All our life is in three: 'Nature, Mercy, Grace.' The high Might of the Trinity is our Father, and the deep Wisdom of the Trinity is our Mother, and the great Love of the Trinity is our Lord"

God, the blessed Trinity, which is everlasting Being, right as He is endless from without beginning, right so it was in His purpose endless, to make Mankind. Which fair Kind first was prepared to His own Son, the Second Person. And when He would, by full accord of all the Trinity, He made us all at once; and in our making He knit us and oned us to Himself: by which oneing we are kept as clear and as noble as we were made. By the virtue of the same precious oneing, we love our Maker and seek Him, praise Him and thank Him, and endlessly enjoy Him. And this is the work which is wrought continually in every soul that shall be saved: which is the Godly Will aforesaid. And thus in our making, God, Almighty, is our Nature's Father; and God, All-Wisdom, is our Nature's Mother; with the Love and the Goodness of the Holy Ghost: which is all one God, one Lord. And in the knitting and the oneing He is our Very, True Spouse, and we His loved Wife, His Fair Maiden: with which Wife He is never displeased. For He saith: I love thee and thou lovest me, and our love shall never be disparted in two.

I beheld the working of all the blessed Trinity: in which beholding I saw and understood these three properties: the property of the Fatherhood, the property of the Motherhood, and the property of the Lordhood, in one God. In our Father Almighty we have our keeping and our bliss as anent our natural Substance, which is to us by our making, without beginning. And in the Second Person in skill and wisdom we have our keeping as anent our Sense-soul: our restoring and our saving; for He is our Mother, Brother, and Saviour. And in our good Lord, the Holy Ghost, we have our rewarding and our meed-giving for our living and our travail, and endless overpassing of all that we desire, in His marvellous courtesy, of His high plenteous grace.

For all our life is in *three*: in the first we have our Being, in the second we have our Increasing, and in the third we have our Fulfilling: the first is Nature, the second is Mercy, and the third is Grace.

For the first, I understood that the high Might of the Trinity is our Father, and the deep Wisdom of the Trinity is our Mother, and the great Love of the Trinity is our Lord: and all this have we in Nature and in the making of our Substance.

And furthermore I saw that the Second Person, which is our Mother as anent the Substance, that same dearworthy Person is become our Mother as anent the Sense-soul. For we are double by God's making: that is to say, Substantial and Sensual. Our Substance is the higher part, which we have in our Father, God Almighty; and the Second Person of the Trinity is our Mother in Nature, in making of our Substance: in whom we are grounded and rooted. And He is our Mother in Mercy, in taking of our Sense-part. And thus our Mother is to us in diverse manners working: in whom our parts are kept undisparted. For in our Mother Christ we profit and increase, and in Mercy He reformeth us and restoreth, and, by the virtue of His Passion and His Death and Uprising, oneth us to our Substance. Thus worketh our Mother in Mercy to all His children which are to Him yielding and obedient.

And Grace worketh with Mercy, and specially in two properties, as it was shewed: which working belongeth to the Third Person, the Holy Ghost. He worketh *rewarding* and *giving*. Rewarding is a large giving-of-truth that the Lord doeth to him that hath travailed; and giving is a courteous working which He doeth freely of Grace, fulfilling and overpassing all that is deserved of creatures.

Thus in our Father, God Almighty, we have our being; and in our Mother of Mercy we have our reforming and restoring: in whom our Parts are oned and all made perfect Man; and by [reward]-yielding and giving in Grace of the Holy Ghost, we are fulfilled.

And our Substance is [in] our Father, God Almighty, and our Substance is [in] our Mother, God, All-wisdom; and our Substance is in our Lord the Holy Ghost, God All-goodness. For our Substance is whole in each Person of the Trinity, which is one God. And our Sense-soul is only in the Second Person Christ Jesus; in whom is the Father and the Holy Ghost: and in Him and by Him we are mightily taken out of Hell, and out of the wretchedness in Earth worshipfully brought up into Heaven and blissfully oned to our Substance: increased in riches and in nobleness by all the virtues of Christ, and by the grace and working of the Holy Ghost.

CHAPTER LIX

"Jesus Christ that doeth Good against evil is our Very Mother: we have our Being of Him where the Ground of Motherhood beginneth,—with all the sweet Keeping by Love, that endlessly followeth."

And all this bliss we have by Mercy and Grace: which manner of bliss we might never have had nor known but if that property of Goodness which is God had been contraried: whereby we have this bliss. For wickedness hath been suffered to rise contrary to the Goodness, and the Goodness of Mercy and Grace contraried against the wickedness and turned all to goodness and to worship, to all these that shall be saved. For it is the property in God which doeth good against evil. Thus Jesus Christ that doeth good against evil is our Very Mother: we have our Being of Him,—where the Ground of Motherhood beginneth,—with all the sweet Keeping of Love that endlessly followeth. As verily as God is our Father, so verily God is our Mother; and that shewed He in all, and especially in these sweet words where He saith: *I it am.* That is to say, *I it am, the Might and the Goodness of the Fatherhood; I it am, the Wisdom of the Motherhood; I it am, the Light and the Grace that is all blessed Love: I it am, the Trinity, I it am, the Unity: I am the sovereign Goodness of all manner of things. I am that maketh thee to love: I am that maketh thee to long: I it am, the endless fulfilling of all true desires.*

For there the soul is highest, noblest, and worthiest, where it is lowest, meekest, and mildest: and [out] of this *Substantial Ground* we have all our virtues in our Sense-part by gift of Nature, by helping and speeding of Mercy and Grace: without the which we may not profit.

Our high Father, God Almighty, which is Being, He knew and loved us from afore any time: of which knowing, in His marvellous deep charity and the foreseeing counsel of all the blessed Trinity, He willed that the Second Person should become our Mother. Our Father [willeth], our Mother worketh, our good Lord the Holy Ghost confirmeth: and therefore it belongeth to us to love our God in whom we have our being: Him reverently thanking and praising for our making, mightily praying to our Mother for mercy and pity, and to our Lord the Holy Ghost for help and grace.

For in these three is all our life: Nature, Mercy, Grace: whereof we have meekness and mildness; patience and pity; and hating of sin and of wickedness,—for it belongeth properly to virtue to hate sin and wickedness. And thus is Jesus our Very Mother in Nature [by virtue] of our first making; and He is our Very Mother in Grace, by taking our nature made. All the fair working, and all the sweet natural office of dearworthy Motherhood is impropriated to the Second Person: for in Him we have this Godly Will whole and safe without end, both in Nature and in Grace, of His own proper Goodness. I understood three manners of beholding of Motherhood in God: the first is grounded in our Nature's *making*; the second is *taking* of our nature,—and there beginneth the Motherhood of Grace; the third is Motherhood of *working*,—and therein is a forthspreading by the same Grace, of length and breadth and height and of deepness without end. And all is one Love.

CHAPTER LX

"The Kind, loving, Mother"

But now behoveth to say a little more of this forthspreading, as I understand in the meaning of our Lord: how that we be brought again by the Motherhood of Mercy and Grace into our Nature's place, where that we were made by the Motherhood of Nature-Love: which kindly-love, it never leaveth us.

Our Kind Mother, our Gracious Mother, for that He would all wholly become our Mother in all things, He took the Ground of His Works full low and full mildly in the Maiden's womb. (And that He shewed in the First [Shewing] where He brought that meek Maid afore the eye of mine understanding in the simple stature as she was when she conceived.) That is to say: our high God is sovereign Wisdom of all: in this low place He arrayed and dight Him full ready in our poor flesh, Himself to do the service and the office of Motherhood in all things.

The Mother's service is nearest, readiest, and surest: [nearest, for it is most of nature; readiest, for it is most of love; and surest] for it is most of truth. This office none might, nor could, nor ever should do to the full, but He alone. We know that all our mothers' bearing is [bearing of] us to pain and to dying: and what is this but that our Very Mother, Jesus, He—All-Love—beareth us to joy and to endless living?— blessed may He be! Thus He sustaineth us within Himself in love; and travailed, unto the full time that He would suffer the sharpest throes and the most grievous pains that ever were or ever shall be; and died at the last. And when He had finished, and so borne us to bliss, yet might not all this make full content to His marvellous love; and that sheweth He in these high overpassing words of love: *If I might suffer more, I would suffer more.*

He might no more die, but He would not stint of working: wherefore then it behoveth Him to feed us; for the dearworthy love of Motherhood hath made Him debtor to us. The mother may give her child suck of her milk, but our precious Mother, Jesus, He may feed us with Himself, and doeth it, full courteously and full tenderly, with the Blessed Sacrament that is precious food of my life; and with all the sweet Sacraments He sustaineth us full mercifully and graciously. And so meant He in this blessed word where that He said: *It is I that*

Holy Church preacheth thee and teacheth thee. That is to say: *All the health and life of Sacraments, all the virtue and grace of my Word, all the Goodness that is ordained in Holy Church for thee, it is I.* The Mother may lay the child tenderly to her breast, but our tender Mother, Jesus, He may homely lead us into His blessed breast, by His sweet open side, and shew therein part of the Godhead and the joys of Heaven, with spiritual sureness of endless bliss. And that shewed He in the Tenth [Shewing], giving the same understanding in this sweet word where He saith: *Lo! how I loved thee*; looking unto [the Wound in] His side, rejoicing.

This fair lovely word *Mother*, it is so sweet and so close in Nature of itself that it may not verily be said of none but of *Him*; and to her that is very Mother of Him and of all. To the property of Motherhood belongeth natural love, wisdom, and knowing; and it is good: for though it be so that our bodily forthbringing be but little, low, and simple in regard of our spiritual forthbringing, yet it is He that doeth it in the creatures by whom that it is done. The Kindly, loving Mother that witteth and knoweth the need of her child, she keepeth it full tenderly, as the nature and condition of Motherhood will. And as it waxeth in age, she changeth her working, but not her love. And when it is waxen of more age, she suffereth that it be beaten in breaking down of vices, to make the child receive virtues and graces. This working, with all that be fair and good, our Lord doeth it in them by whom it is done: thus He is our Mother in Nature by the working of Grace in the lower part for love of the higher part. And He willeth that we know this: for He will have all our love fastened to Him. And in this I saw that all our duty that we owe, by God's bidding, to Fatherhood and Motherhood, for [reason of] God's Fatherhood and Motherhood is fulfilled in true loving of God; which blessed love Christ worketh in us. And this was shewed in all [the Revelations] and especially in the high plenteous words where He saith: *It is I that thou lovest.*

CHAPTER LXI

"By the assay of this falling we shall have an high marvellous
knowing of Love in God, without end. For strong and marvellous is
that love which may not, nor will not, be broken for trespass"

And in our spiritual forthbringing He useth more tenderness of
keeping, without any likeness: by as much as our soul is of more price
in His sight. He kindleth our understanding, He directeth our ways,
He easeth our conscience, He comforteth our soul, He lighteneth our
heart, and giveth us, in part, knowing and believing in His blissful
Godhead, with gracious mind in His sweet Manhood and His blessed
Passion, with reverent marvelling in His high, overpassing Goodness;
and maketh us to love all that He loveth, for His love, and to be well-
pleased with Him and all His works. And when we fall, hastily He
raiseth us by His lovely calling and gracious touching. And when we
be thus strengthened by His sweet working, then we with all our will
choose Him, by His sweet grace, to be His servants and His lovers
lastingly without end.

And after this He suffereth some of us to fall more hard and more
grievously than ever we did afore, as us thinketh. And then ween we
(who be not all wise) that all were nought that we have begun. But this
is not so. For it needeth us to fall, and it needeth us to see it. For if we
never fell, we should not know how feeble and how wretched we are
of our self, and also we should not fully know that marvellous love of
our Maker. For we shall see verily in heaven, without end, that we
have grievously sinned in this life, and notwithstanding this, we shall
see that we were never hurt in His love, we were never the less of
price in His sight. And by the assay of this falling we shall have an high,
marvellous knowing of love in God, without end. For strong and
marvellous is that love which may not, nor will not, be broken for
trespass. And this is one understanding of [our] profit. Another is the
lowness and meekness that we shall get by the sight of our falling: for
thereby we shall highly be raised in heaven; to which raising we might
never have come without that meekness. And therefore it needeth us
to see it; and if we see it not, though we fell it should not profit us.
And commonly, first we fall and later we see it: and both of the Mercy
of God.

The mother may suffer the child to fall sometimes, and to be hurt in
diverse manners for its own profit, but she may never suffer that any

manner of peril come to the child, for love. And though our earthly mother may suffer her child to perish, our heavenly Mother, Jesus, may not suffer us that are His children to perish: for He is All-mighty, All-wisdom, and All-love; and so is none but He,—blessed may He be!

But oftentimes when our falling and our wretchedness is shewed us, we are so sore adread, and so greatly ashamed of our self, that scarcely we find where we may hold us. But then willeth not our courteous Mother that we flee away, for Him were nothing lother. But He willeth then that we use the condition of a child: for when it is hurt, or adread, it runneth hastily to the mother for help, with all its might. So willeth He that we do, as a meek child saying thus: *My kind Mother, my Gracious Mother, my dearworthy Mother, have mercy on me: I have made myself foul and unlike to Thee, and I nor may nor can amend it but with thine help and grace.* And if we feel us not then eased forthwith, be we sure that He useth the condition of a wise mother. For if He see that it be more profit to us to mourn and to weep, He suffereth it, with ruth and pity, unto the best time, for love. And He willeth then that we use the property of a child, that evermore of nature trusteth to the love of the mother in weal and in woe.

And He willeth that we take us mightily to the Faith of Holy Church and find there our dearworthy Mother, in solace of true Understanding, with all the blessed Common. For one single person may oftentimes be broken, as it seemeth to himself, but the whole Body of Holy Church was never broken, nor never shall be, without end. And therefore a sure thing it is, a good and a gracious, to will meekly and mightily to be fastened and oned to our Mother, Holy Church, that is, Christ Jesus. For the food of mercy that is His dearworthy blood and precious water is plenteous to make us fair and clean; the blessed wounds of our Saviour be open and enjoy to heal us; the sweet, gracious hands of our Mother be ready and diligently about us. For He in all this working useth the office of a kind nurse that hath nought else to do but to give heed about the salvation of her child.

It is His office to save us: it is His worship to do [for] us, and it is His will [that] we know it: for He willeth that we love Him sweetly and trust in Him meekly and mightily. And this shewed He in these gracious words: *I keep thee full surely.*

CHAPTER LXII

"God is Very Father and Very Mother of Nature: and all natures that He hath made to flow out of Him to work His will shall be restored and brought again into Him by the salvation of Mankind through the working of Grace"

For in that time He shewed our frailty and our fallings, our afflictings and our settings at nought, our despites and our outcastings, and all our woe so far forth as methought it might befall in this life. And therewith He shewed His blessed Might, His blessed Wisdom, His blessed Love: that He keepeth us in this time as tenderly and as sweetly to His worship, and as surely to our salvation, as He doeth when we are in most solace and comfort. And thereto He raiseth us spiritually and highly in heaven, and turneth it all to His worship and to our joy, without end. For His love suffereth us never to lose time.

And all this is of the Nature-Goodness of God, by the working of Grace. God is Nature in His being: that is to say, that Goodness that is Nature, it is God. He is the ground, He is the substance, He is the same thing that is Nature-hood. And He is very Father and very Mother of Nature: and all natures that He hath made to flow out of Him to work His will shall be restored and brought again into Him by the salvation of man through the working of Grace.

For of all natures that He hath set in diverse creatures by part, in man is all the whole; in fulness and in virtue, in fairness and in goodness, in royalty and nobleness, in all manner of majesty, of preciousness and worship. Here may we see that we are all beholden to God for nature, and we are all beholden to God for grace. Here may we see us needeth not greatly to seek far out to know sundry natures, but to Holy Church, unto our Mother's breast: that is to say, unto our own soul where our Lord dwelleth; and there shall we find all now in faith and in understanding. And afterward verily in Himself clearly, in bliss.

But let no man nor woman take this singularly to himself: for it is not so, it is general: for it is [of] our precious Christ, and to Him was this fair nature adight for the worship and nobility of man's making, and for the joy and the bliss of man's salvation; even as He saw, wist, and knew from without beginning.

CHAPTER LXIII

"As verily as sin is unclean, so verily is it unkind"—a disease or
monstrous thing against nature. "He shall heal us full fair."

Here may we see that we have verily of Nature to hate sin, and we
have verily of Grace to hate sin. For Nature is all good and fair in itself,
and Grace was sent out to save Nature and destroy sin, and bring again
fair nature to the blessed point from whence it came: that is God; with
more nobleness and worship by the virtuous working of Grace. For it
shall be seen afore God by all His Holy in joy without end that Nature
hath been assayed in the fire of tribulation and therein hath been
found no flaw, no fault. Thus are Nature and Grace of one accord: for
Grace is God, as Nature is God: He is two in manner of working and
one in love; and neither of these worketh without other: they be not
disparted.

And when we by Mercy of God and with His help accord us to Nature
and Grace, we shall see verily that sin is in sooth viler and more
painful than hell, without likeness: for it is contrary to our fair nature.
For as verily as sin is unclean, so verily is it unnatural, and thus an
horrible thing to see for the loved soul that would be all fair and
shining in the sight of God, as Nature and Grace teacheth.

Yet be we not adread of this, save inasmuch as dread may speed us:
but meekly make we our moan to our dearworthy Mother, and He
shall besprinkle us in His precious blood and make our soul full soft
and full mild, and heal us full fair by process of time, right as it is most
worship to Him and joy to us without end. And of this sweet fair
working He shall never cease nor stint till all His dearworthy children
be born and forthbrought. (And that shewed He where He shewed
[me] understanding of the ghostly Thirst, that is the love-longing that
shall last till Doomsday.)

Thus in [our] Very Mother, Jesus, our life is grounded, in the
foreseeing Wisdom of Himself from without beginning, with the high
Might of the Father, the high sovereign Goodness of the Holy Ghost.
And in the taking of our nature He quickened us; in His blessed dying
upon the Cross He bare us to endless life; and from that time, and now,
and evermore unto Doomsday, He feedeth us and furthereth us: even
as that high sovereign Kindness of Motherhood, and as Kindly need
of Childhood asketh.

Fair and sweet is our Heavenly Mother in the sight of our souls; precious and lovely are the Gracious Children in the sight of our Heavenly Mother, with mildness and meekness, and all the fair virtues that belong to children in Nature. For of nature the Child despaireth not of the Mother's love, of nature the Child presumeth not of itself, of nature the Child loveth the Mother and each one of the other [children]. These are the fair virtues, with all other that be like, wherewith our Heavenly Mother is served and pleased.

And I understood none higher stature in this life than Childhood, in feebleness and failing of might and of wit, unto the time that our Gracious Mother hath brought us up to our Father's Bliss. And then shall it verily be known to us His meaning in those sweet words where He saith: *All shall be well: and thou shalt see, thyself, that all manner of things shall be well.* And then shall the Bliss of our Mother, in Christ, be new to begin in the Joys of our God: which new beginning shall last without end, new beginning.

Thus I understood that all His blessed children which be come out of Him by Nature shall be brought again into Him by Grace.

THE FIFTEENTH REVELATION

CHAPTER LXIV

"Thou shalt come up above." "A very fair creature, a little Child—
nimble and lively, whiter than lily"

Afore this time I had great longing and desire of God's gift to be delivered of this world and of this life. For oftentimes I beheld the woe that is here, and the weal and the bliss that is being there: (and if there had been no pain in this life but the absence of our Lord, methought it was some-time more than I might bear;) and this made me to mourn, and eagerly to long. And also from mine own wretchedness, sloth, and weakness, me liked not to live and to travail, as me fell to do.

And to all this our courteous Lord answered for comfort and patience, and said these words: *Suddenly thou shalt be taken from all thy pain, from all thy sickness, from all thy distress and from all thy woe. And thou shalt come up above and thou shalt have me to thy meed, and thou shalt be fulfilled of love and of bliss. And thou shalt never have no manner of pain, no manner of misliking, no wanting of will; but ever joy and bliss without end. What should it then aggrieve thee to suffer awhile, seeing that it is my will and my worship?*

And in this word: *Suddenly thou shalt be taken,*—I saw that God rewardeth man for the patience that he hath in abiding God's will, and for his time, and [for] that man lengtheneth his patience over the time of his living. For not-knowing of his time of passing, that is a great profit: for if a man knew his time, he should not have patience over that time; but, as God willeth, while the soul is in the body it seemeth to itself that it is ever at the point to be taken. For all this life and this languor that we have here is but a point, and when we are taken suddenly out of pain into bliss then pain shall be nought.

And in this time I saw a body lying on the earth, which body shewed heavy and horrible, without shape and form, as it were a swollen quag of stinking mire. And suddenly out of this body sprang a full fair creature, a little Child, fully shapen and formed, nimble and lively, whiter than lily; which swiftly glided up into heaven. And the swollenness of the body betokeneth great wretchedness of our deadly flesh, and the littleness of the Child betokeneth the cleanness of purity in the soul. And methought: *With this body abideth no fairness of this Child, and on this Child dwelleth no foulness of this body.*

It is more blissful that man be taken from pain, than that pain be taken from man; for if pain be taken from us it may come again: therefore it is a sovereign comfort and blissful beholding in a loving soul that we shall be taken from pain. For in this behest I saw a marvellous compassion that our Lord hath in us for our woe, and a courteous promising of clear deliverance. For He willeth that we be comforted in the overpassing; and *that* He shewed in these words: *And thou shalt come up above, and thou shalt have me to thy meed, and thou shalt be fulfilled of joy and bliss.*

It is God's will that we set the point of our thought in this blissful beholding as often as we may,—and as long time keep us therein with His grace; for this is a blessed contemplation to the soul that is led of God, and full greatly to His worship, for the time that it lasteth. And [when] we fall again to our heaviness, and spiritual blindness, and feeling of pains spiritual and bodily, by our frailty, it is God's will that we know that He hath not forgotten us. And so signifieth He in these words: *And thou shalt never more have pain; no manner of sickness, no manner of misliking, no wanting of will; but ever joy and bliss without end. What should it then aggrieve thee to suffer awhile, seeing it is my will and my worship?*

It is God's will that we take His behests and His comfortings as largely and as mightily as we may take them, and also He willeth that we take our abiding and our troubles as lightly as we may take them, and set them at nought. For the more lightly we take them, and the less price we set on them, for love, the less pain we shall have in the feeling of them, and the more thanks and meed we shall have for them.

CHAPTER LXV

"The Charity of God maketh in us such a unity that, when it is truly seen, no man can part himself from other"

And thus I understood that what man or woman with firm will chooseth God in this life, for love, he may be sure that he is loved without end: which endless love worketh in him that grace. For He willeth that we be as assured in hope of the bliss of heaven while we are here, as we shall be in sureness while we are there. And ever the more pleasance and joy that we take in this sureness, with reverence and meekness, the better pleaseth Him, as it was shewed. This reverence that I mean is a holy courteous dread of our Lord, to which meekness is united: and that is, that a creature seeth the Lord marvellous great, and itself marvellous little. For these virtues are had endlessly by the loved of God, and this may now be seen and felt in measure through the gracious presence of our Lord when it is [seen]: which presence in all things is most desired, for it worketh marvellous assuredness in true faith, and sure hope, by greatness of charity, in dread that is sweet and delectable.

It is God's will that I see myself as much bound to Him in love as if He had done for me all that He hath done; and thus should every soul think inwardly of its Lover. That is to say, the Charity of God maketh in us such a unity that, when it is truly seen, no man can part himself from other. And thus ought our soul to think that God hath done for it all that He hath done.

And this sheweth He to make us to love Him and nought dread but Him. For it is His will that we perceive that all the might of our Enemy is taken into our Friend's hand; and therefore the soul that knoweth assuredly this, he shall not dread but Him that he loveth. All other dread he setteth among passions and bodily sickness and imaginations. And therefore though we be in so much pain, woe, and distress that it seemeth to us we can think [of] right nought but [of] that [which] we are in, or [of] that [which] we feel, [yet] as soon as we may, pass we lightly over, and set we it at nought. And why? For that God willeth we know [Him]; and if we know Him and love Him and reverently dread Him, we shall have peace, and be in great rest, and it shall be great pleasance to us, all that He doeth. And this shewed our Lord in these words: *What should it then aggrieve thee to suffer awhile, sith it is my will and my worship?*

Now have I told you of Fifteen Revelations, as God vouchsafed to minister them to [my] mind, renewed by lightings and touchings, I hope of the same Spirit that shewed them all.

Of which Fifteen Shewings the First began early in the morn, about the hour of four; and they lasted, shewing by process full fair and steadily, each following other, till it was nine of the day, overpassed.

CHAPTER LXVI

"All was closed, and I saw no more." "For the folly of feeling a little bodily pain I unwisely lost for the time the comfort of all this blessed Shewing of our Lord God"

And after this the good Lord shewed the Sixteenth [Revelation] on the night following, as I shall tell after: which Sixteenth was conclusion and confirmation to all Fifteen.

But first me behoveth to tell you as anent my feebleness, wretchedness and blindness.—I have said in the beginning: *And in this [moment] all my pain was suddenly taken from me:* of which pain I had no grief nor distress as long as the Fifteen Shewings lasted following. And at the end all was close, and I saw no more. And soon I felt that I should live and languish; and anon my sickness came again: first in my head with a sound and a din, and suddenly all my body was fulfilled with sickness like as it was afore. And I was as barren and as dry as [if] I never had comfort but little. And as a wretched creature I moaned and cried for feeling of my bodily pains and for failing of comfort, spiritual and bodily.

Then came a Religious person to me and asked me how I fared. I said I had raved to-day. And he laughed loud and heartily. And I said: *The Cross that stood afore my face, methought it bled fast.* And with this word the person that I spake to waxed all sober and marvelled. And anon I was sore ashamed and astonished for my recklessness, and I thought: *This man taketh in sober earnest the least word that I might say.* Then said I no more thereof. And when I saw that he took it earnestly and with so great reverence, I wept, full greatly ashamed, and would have been shriven; but at that time I could tell it no priest, for I thought: *How should a priest believe me? I believe not our Lord God.* This [Shewing] I believed verily for the time that I saw Him, and so was then my will and my meaning ever for to do without end; but as a fool I let it pass from my mind. Ah! lo, wretch that I am! this was a great sin, great unkindness, that I for folly of feeling of a little bodily pain, so unwisely lost for the time the comfort of all this blessed Shewing of our Lord God. Here may you see what I am of myself.

But herein would our Courteous Lord not leave me. And I lay still till night, trusting in His mercy, and then I began to sleep. And in the sleep, at the beginning, methought the Fiend set him on my throat, putting forth a visage full near my face, like a young man's and it was long and wondrous lean: I saw never none such. The colour was red like the tilestone when it is new-burnt, with black spots therein like black freckles—fouler than the tilestone. His hair was red as rust, clipped in front, with full locks hanging on the temples. He grinned on me with a malicious semblance, shewing white teeth: and so much methought it the more horrible. Body nor hands had he none shapely, but with his paws he held me in the throat, and would have strangled me, but he might not.

This horrible Shewing was made [whilst I was] sleeping, and so was none other. But in all this time I trusted to be saved and kept by the mercy of God. And our Courteous Lord gave me grace to waken; and scarcely had I my life. The persons that were with me looked on me, and wet my temples, and my heart began to comfort. And anon a light smoke came in the door, with a great heat and a foul stench. I said: *Benedicite Domine! it is all on fire that is here!* And I weened it had been a bodily fire that should have burnt us all to death. I asked them that were with me if they felt any stench. They said, Nay: they felt none. I said: *Blessed be God!* For then wist I well it was the Fiend that was come to tempest me. And anon I took to that [which] our Lord had shewed me on the same day, with all the Faith of Holy Church (for I beheld it is both one), and fled thereto as to my comfort. And anon all vanished away, and I was brought to great rest and peace, without sickness of body or dread of conscience.

THE SIXTEENTH REVELATION

CHAPTER LXVII

"The place that Jesus taketh in our soul He shall never remove from, without end:—for in us His homliest home and His endless dwelling." "Our soul can never have rest in things that are beneath itself—yet may it not abide in the beholding of its self"

And then our Lord opened my spiritual eye and shewed me my soul in midst of my heart. I saw the Soul so large as it were an endless world, and as it were a blissful kingdom. And by the conditions that I saw therein I understood that it is a worshipful City. In the midst of that City sitteth our Lord Jesus, God and Man, a fair Person of large stature, highest Bishop, most majestic King, most worshipful Lord; and I saw Him clad majestically. And worshipfully He sitteth in the Soul, even-right in peace and rest. And the Godhead ruleth and sustaineth heaven and earth and all that is,—sovereign Might, sovereign Wisdom, and sovereign Goodness,—[but] the place that Jesus taketh in *our Soul* He shall never remove it, without end, as to my sight: for in us is His *homliest* home and His *endless* dwelling.

And in this [sight] He shewed the satisfying that He hath of the making of Man's Soul. For as well as the Father might make a creature, and as well as the Son could make a creature, so well would the Holy Ghost that Man's Soul were made: and so it was done. And therefore the blessed Trinity enjoyeth without end in the making of Man's Soul: for He saw from without beginning what should please Him without end. All thing that He hath made sheweth His Lordship,—as understanding was given at the same time by example of a creature that is to see great treasures and kingdoms belonging to a lord; and when it had seen all the nobleness beneath, then, marvelling, it was moved to seek above to the high place where the lord dwelleth, knowing, by reason, that his dwelling is in the worthiest place. And thus I understood in verity that our Soul may never have rest in things that are beneath itself. And when it cometh above all creatures into the Self, yet may it not abide in the beholding of its Self, but all the beholding is blissfully set in God that is the Maker dwelling therein. For in Man's Soul is His very dwelling; and the highest light and the brightest shining of the City is the glorious love of our Lord, as to my sight.

And what may make us more to enjoy in God than to see in Him that He enjoyeth in the highest of all His works? For I saw in the same Shewing that if the blessed Trinity might have made Man's Soul any better, any fairer, any nobler than it was made, He should not have been full pleased with the making of Man's Soul. And He willeth that our hearts be mightily raised above the deepness of the earth and all vain sorrows, and rejoice in Him.

CHAPTER LXVIII

"He said not: *Thou shalt not be tempested, thou shalt not be travailed, thou shalt not be afflicted*; but He said: *Thou shalt not be overcome*"

This was a delectable Sight and a restful Shewing, that it is so *without end*. The beholding of this while we are here is full pleasing to God and full great profit to us; and the soul that thus beholdeth, it maketh it like to Him that is beheld, and oneth it in rest and peace by His grace. And this was a singular joy and bliss to me that I saw Him *sitting*: for the [quiet] secureness of sitting sheweth endless dwelling.

And He gave me to know soothfastly that it was He that shewed me all afore. And when I had beheld this with heedfulness, then shewed our good Lord words full meekly without voice and without opening of lips, right as He had [afore] done, and said full sweetly: *Wit it now well that it was no raving that thou sawest to-day: but take it and believe it, and keep thee therein, and comfort thee therewith, and trust thou thereto: and thou shalt not be overcome.*

These Last Words were said for believing and true sureness that it is our Lord Jesus that shewed me all. And right as in the first word that our good Lord shewed, signifying His blissful Passion,—*Herewith is the devil overcome,*—right so He said in the last word, with full true secureness, meaning us all: *Thou shalt not* be overcome. And all this teaching in this true comfort, it is general, to all mine even-Christians, as it is aforesaid: and so is God's will.

And this word: *Thou shalt not be overcome*, was said full clearly and full mightily, for assuredness and comfort against all tribulations that may come. He said not: *Thou shalt not be tempested, thou shall not be travailed, thou shah not be afflicted*; but He said: *Thou shalt not be overcome.* God willeth that we take heed to these words, and that we be ever strong in sure trust, in weal and woe. For He loveth and enjoyeth us, and so willeth He that we love and enjoy Him and mightily trust in Him; and *all shall be well.*

And soon after, all was close and I saw no more.

CHAPTER LXIX

"I was delivered from the Enemy by the virtue of Christ's Passion"

After this the Fiend came again with his heat and with his stench, and gave me much ado, the stench was so vile and so painful, and also dreadful and travailous. Also I heard a bodily jangling, as if it had been of two persons; and both, to my thinking, jangled at one time as if they had holden a parliament with a great busy-ness; and all was soft muttering, so that I understood nought that they said. And all this was to stir me to despair, as methought,—seeming to me as [though] they mocked at praying of prayers which are said boisterously with [the] mouth, failing [of] devout attending and wise diligence: the which we owe to God in our prayers.

And our Lord God gave me grace mightily for to trust in Him, and to comfort my soul with bodily speech as I should have done to another person that had been travailed. Methought *that* busy-ness might not be likened to no bodily busy-ness. My bodily eye I set in the same Cross where I had been in comfort afore that time; my tongue with speech of Christ's Passion and rehearsing the Faith of Holy Church; and my heart to fasten on God with all the trust and the might. And I thought to myself, saying: *Thou hast now great busy-ness to keep thee in the Faith for that thou shouldst not be taken of the Enemy: wouldst thou now from this time evermore be so busy to keep thee from sin, this were a good and a sovereign occupation!* For I thought in sooth were I safe from sin, I were full safe from all the fiends of hell and enemies of my soul.

And thus he occupied me all that night, and on the morn till it was about prime day. And anon they were all gone, and all passed; and they left nothing but stench, and that lasted still awhile; and I scorned him.

And thus was I delivered from him by the virtue of Christ's Passion: for *therewith is the Fiend overcome*, as our Lord Jesus Christ said afore.

CHAPTER LXX

"Above the Faith is no goodness kept in this life, as to my sight, and beneath the Faith is no help of soul; but *in* the Faith, *there* willeth the Lord that we keep us"

In all this blessed Shewing our good Lord gave understanding that the Sight should pass: which blessed Shewing the Faith keepeth, with His own good will and His grace. For He left with me neither sign nor token whereby I might know it, but He left with me His own blessed word in true understanding, bidding me full mightily that I should believe it. And so I do,—Blessed may He be!—I believe that He is our Saviour that shewed it, and that it is the Faith that He shewed: and therefore I believe it, rejoicing. And thereto I am bounden by all His own meaning, with the next words that follow: *Keep thee therein, and comfort thee therewith, and trust thou thereto.*

Thus I am bounden to keep it in my faith. For on the same day that it was shewed, what time that the Sight was passed, as a wretch I forsook it, and openly I said that I had raved. Then our Lord Jesus of His mercy would not let it perish, but He showed it all again *within in my soul* with more fulness, with the blessed light of His precious love: saying these words full mightily and full meekly: *Wit it now well: it was no raving that thou sawest this day.* As if He had said: *For that the Sight was passed from thee, thou losedst it and hadst not skill to keep it. But wit it now*; that is to say, *now that thou seest it.* This was said not only for that same time, but also to set thereupon the ground of my faith when He saith anon following: *But take it, believe it, and keep thee therein and comfort thee therewith and trust thou thereto; and thou shalt not be overcome.*

In these six words that follow (*Take it*—[etc.]) His meaning is to fasten it faithfully in our heart: for He willeth that it dwell with us in faith to our life's end, and after in fulness of joy, desiring that we have ever steadfast trust in His blissful behest—knowing His Goodness.

For our faith is contraried in diverse manners by our own blindness, and our spiritual enemy, within and without; and therefore our precious Lover helpeth us with spiritual sight and true teaching in sundry manners within and without, whereby that we may know Him. And therefore in whatsoever manner He teacheth us, He willeth that we perceive Him wisely, receive Him sweetly, and keep us in Him faithfully. For above the Faith is no goodness kept in this life, as to my sight, and beneath the Faith is no help of soul; but in the Faith, there willeth the Lord that we keep us. For we have by His goodness and His own working to keep us in the Faith; and by His sufferance through ghostly enmity we are assayed in the Faith and made mighty. For if our faith had none enmity, it should deserve no meed, according to the understanding that I have in all our Lord's teaching.

CHAPTER LXXI

"Three manners of looking seen in our Lord's Countenance"

Glad and joyous and sweet is the Blissful lovely Cheer of our Lord to our souls. For He [be]holdeth us ever, living in love-longing: and He willeth that *our* soul be in glad cheer to Him, to give Him His meed. And thus, I hope, with His grace He hath [drawn], and more shall draw, the Outer Cheer to the Inner Cheer, and make us all one with Him, and each of us with other, in true lasting joy that is Jesus.

I have signifying of Three manners of Cheer of our Lord. The first is Cheer of Passion, as He shewed while He was here in this life, dying. Though this [manner of] Beholding be mournful and troubled, yet it is glad and joyous: for He is God.—The second manner of Cheer is [of] Ruth and Compassion: and this sheweth He, with sureness of Keeping, to all His lovers that betake them to His mercy. The third is the Blissful Cheer, as it shall be without end: and this was [shewed] oftenest and longest-continued.

And thus in the time of our pain and our woe He sheweth us Cheer of His Passion and His Cross, helping us to bear it by His own blessed virtue. And in the time of our sinning He sheweth to us Cheer of Ruth and Pity, mightily keeping us and defending us against all our enemies. And these be the common Cheer which He sheweth to us in this life; therewith mingling the third: and that is His Blissful Cheer, like, in part, as it shall be in Heaven. And that [shewing is] by gracious touching and sweet lighting of the spiritual life, whereby that we are kept in sure faith, hope, and charity, with contrition and devotion, and also with contemplation and all manner of true solace and sweet comforts.

CHAPTER LXXII

"As long as we be meddling with any part of sin we shall never see clearly the Blissful Countenance of our Lord"

But now behoveth me to tell in what manner I saw sin deadly in the creatures which shall not die for sin, but live in the joy of God without end.

I saw that two contrary things should never be together in one place. The most contrary that are, is the highest bliss and the deepest pain. The highest bliss that is, is to have Him in clarity of endless life, Him verily seeing, Him sweetly feeling, all-perfectly having in fulness of joy. And thus was the Blissful Cheer of our Lord shewed in Pity: in which Shewing I saw that sin is most contrary,—so far forth that as long as we be meddling with any part of sin, we shall never see clearly the Blissful Cheer of our Lord. And the more horrible and grievous that our sins be, the deeper are we for that time from this blissful sight. And therefore it seemeth to us oftentimes as we were in peril of death, in a part of hell, for the sorrow and pain that the sin is to us. And thus we are dead for the time from the very sight of our blissful life. But in all this I saw soothfastly that we be not dead in the sight of God, nor He passeth never from us. But He shall never have His full bliss in us till we have our full bliss in Him, verily seeing His fair Blissful Cheer. For we are ordained thereto in nature, and get thereto by grace. Thus I saw how sin is deadly for a short time in the blessed creatures of endless life.

And ever the more clearly that the soul seeth this Blissful Cheer by grace of loving, the more it longeth to see it in fulness. For notwithstanding that our Lord God dwelleth in us and is here with us, and albeit He claspeth us and encloseth us for tender love that He may never leave us, and is more near to us than tongue can tell or heart can think, yet may we never stint of moaning nor of weeping nor of longing till when we see Him clearly in His Blissful

Countenance. For in that precious blissful sight there may no woe abide, nor any weal fail.

And in this I saw matter of mirth and matter of moaning: matter of mirth: for our Lord, our Maker, is so near to us, and in us, and we in Him, by sureness of keeping through His great goodness; matter of moaning: for our ghostly eye is so blind and we be so borne down by weight of our mortal flesh and darkness of sin, that we may not see our Lord God clearly in His fair Blissful Cheer. No; and because of this dimness scarsely we can believe and trust His great love and our sureness of keeping. And therefore it is that I say we may never stint of moaning nor of weeping. This "weeping" meaneth not all in pouring out of tears by our bodily eye, but also hath more ghostly understanding. For the kindly desire of our soul is so great and so unmeasurable, that if there were given us for our solace and for our comfort all the noble things that ever God made in heaven and in earth, and we saw not the fair Blissful Cheer of Himself, yet we should not stint of moaning nor ghostly weeping, that is to say, of painful longing, till when we [should] see verily the fair Blissful Cheer of our Maker. And if we were in all the pain that heart can think and tongue may tell, if we might in that time see His fair Blissful Cheer, all this pain should not aggrieve us.

Thus is that Blissful Sight [the] end of all manner of pain to the loving soul, and the fulfilling of all manner of joy and bliss. And that shewed He in the high, marvellous words where He said: *I it am that is highest; I it am that is lowest; I it am that is all.*

It belongeth to us to have three manner of knowings: the first is that we know our Lord God; the second is that we know our self: what we are by Him, in Nature and Grace; the third is that we know meekly what our self is anent our sin and feebleness. And for these three was all the Shewing made, as to mine understanding.

CHAPTER LXXIII

"Two manners of sickness that we have: impatience, or sloth;—
despair, or mistrustful dread"

All the blessed teaching of our Lord was shewed by three parts: that is to say, by bodily sight, and by word formed in mine understanding, and by spiritual sight. For the bodily sight, I have said as I saw, as truly as I can; and for the words, I have said them right as our Lord shewed them to me; and for the spiritual sight, I have told some deal, but I may never fully tell it: and therefore of this sight I am stirred to say more, as God will give me grace.

God shewed two manners of sickness that we have: the one is impatience, or sloth: for we bear our travail and our pains heavily; the other is despair, or doubtful dread, which I shall speak of after. *Generally*, He shewed *sin*, wherein that all is comprehended, but in special He shewed only these two. And these two are they that most do travail and tempest us, according to that which our Lord shewed me; and of them He would have us be amended. I speak of such men and women as for God's love hate sin and dispose themselves to do God's will: then by our spiritual blindness and bodily heaviness we are most inclining to these. And therefore it is God's will that they be known, for then we shall refuse them as we do other sins.

And for help of this, full meekly our Lord shewed the patience that He had in His Hard Passion; and also the joying and the satisfying that He hath of that Passion, for love. And this He shewed in example that we should gladly and wisely bear our pains, for that is great pleasing to Him and endless profit to us. And the cause why we are travailed with them is for lack in knowing of Love. Though the three Persons in the Trinity be all even in Itself, the soul took most understanding in Love; yea, and He willeth that in all things we have our beholding and our enjoying in Love. And of this knowing are we most blind. For some of us believe that God is Almighty and may do all, and that He is All-Wisdom and can do all; but that He is All-Love and will do all, there we stop short. And this not-knowing it is, that hindereth most God's lovers, as to my sight.

For when we begin to hate sin, and amend us by the ordinance of Holy Church, yet there dwelleth a dread that letteth us, because of the beholding of our self and of our sins afore done. And some of us because of our every-daily sins: for we hold not our Covenants, nor keep we our cleanness that our Lord setteth us in, but fall oftentimes into so much wretchedness that shame it is to see it. And the beholding of this maketh us so sorry and so heavy, that scarsely we can find any comfort.

And this dread we take sometime for a meekness, but it is a foul blindness and a weakness. And we cannot despise it as we do another sin, that we know [as sin]: for it cometh [subtly] of Enmity, and it is against truth. For it is God's will that of all the properties of the blissful Trinity, we should have most sureness and comfort in Love: for Love maketh Might and Wisdom full meek to us. For right as by the courtesy of God He forgiveth our sin after the time that we repent us, right so willeth He that *we* forgive our sin, as anent our unskilful heaviness and our doubtful dreads.

CHAPTER LXXIV

"There is no dread that fully pleaseth God in us but reverent dread"

For I understand [that there be] four manner of dreads. One is the dread of an affright that cometh to a man suddenly by frailty. This dread doeth good, for it helpeth to purge man, as doeth bodily sickness or such other pain as is not sin. For all such pains help man if they be patiently taken. The second is dread of pain, whereby man is stirred and wakened from sleep of sin. He is not able for the time to perceive the soft comfort of the Holy Ghost, till he have understanding of this dread of pain, of bodily death, of spiritual enemies; and this dread stirreth us to seek comfort and mercy of God, and thus this dread helpeth us, and enableth us to have contrition by the blissful touching of the Holy Ghost. The third is doubtful dread. Doubtful dread in as much as it draweth to despair, God will have it turned in us into love by the knowing of love: that is to say, that the bitterness of doubt be turned into the sweetness of natural love by grace. For it may never please our Lord that His servants doubt in His Goodness. The fourth is reverent dread: for there is no dread that fully pleaseth God in us but reverent dread. And that is full soft, for the more it is had, the less it is felt for sweetness of love.

Love and Dread are brethren, and they are rooted in us by the Goodness of our Maker, and they shall never be taken from us without end. We have of nature to love and we have of grace to love: and we have of nature to dread and we have of grace to dread. It belongeth to the Lordship and to the Fatherhood to be dreaded, as it belongeth to the Goodness to be loved: and it belongeth to us that are His servants and His children to dread Him for Lordship and Fatherhood, as it belongeth to us to love Him for Goodness.

And though this reverent-dread and love be not parted asunder, yet they are not both one, but they are two in property and in working, and neither of them may be had without other. Therefore I am sure, he that loveth, he dreadeth, though that he feel it but a little.

All dreads other than reverent dread that are proffered to us, though they come under the colour of holiness yet are not so true, and hereby may they be known asunder.—That dread that maketh us hastily to flee from all that is not good and fall into our Lord's breast, as the Child into the Mother's bosom, with all our intent and with all our mind, knowing our feebleness and our great need, knowing His everlasting goodness and His blissful love, only seeking to Him for salvation, cleaving to [Him] with sure trust: that dread that bringeth us into this working, it is natural, gracious, good and true. And all that is contrary to this, either it is wrong, or it is mingled with wrong. Then is this the remedy, to know them both and refuse the wrong.

For the natural property of dread which we have in this life by the gracious working of the Holy Ghost, the same shall be in heaven afore God, gentle, courteous, and full delectable. And thus we shall in love be homely and near to God, and we shall in dread be gentle and courteous to God: and both alike equal.

Desire we of our Lord God to dread Him reverently, to love Him meekly, to trust in Him mightily; for when we dread Him reverently and love Him meekly our trust is never in vain. For the more that we trust, and the more mightily, the more we please and worship our Lord that we trust in. And if we fail in this reverent dread and meek love (as God forbid we should!), our trust shall soon be misruled for the time. And therefore it needeth us much to pray our Lord of grace that we may have this reverent dread and meek love, of His gift, in heart and in work. For without this, no man may please God.

CHAPTER LXXV

"We shall see verily the cause of all things that He hath done; and evermore we shall see the cause of all things that He hath permitted"

I saw that God can do all that we need. And these three that I shall speak of we need: love, longing, pity. Pity in love keepeth us in the time of our need; and longing in the same love draweth us up into Heaven. For the Thirst of God is to have the general Man unto Him: in which thirst He hath drawn His Holy that be now in bliss; and getting His lively members, ever He draweth and drinketh, and yet He thirsteth and longeth.

I saw three manners of longing in God, and all to one end; of which we have the same in us, and by the same virtue and for the same end.

The first is, that He longeth to teach us to know Him and love Him evermore, as it is convenient and speedful to us. The second is, that He longeth to have us up to His Bliss, as souls are when they are taken out of pain into Heaven. The third is to fulfill us in bliss; and that shall be on the Last Day, fulfilled ever to last. For I saw, as it is known in our Faith, that the pain and the sorrow shall be ended to all that shall be saved. And not only we shall receive the same bliss that souls afore have had in heaven, but also we shall receive a new [bliss], which plenteously shall be flowing out of God into us and shall fulfill us; and these be the goods which He hath ordained to give us from without beginning. These goods are treasured and hid in Himself; for unto that time [no] Creature is mighty nor worthy to receive them.

In this [fulfilling] we shall see verily the cause of all things that He hath done; and evermore we shall see the cause of all things that He hath suffered. And the bliss and the fulfilling shall be so deep and so high that, for wonder and marvel, all creatures shall have to God so great reverent dread, overpassing that which hath been seen and felt before, that the pillars of heaven shall tremble and quake. But this manner of trembling and dread shall have no pain; but it belongeth to the worthy might of God thus to be beholden by His creatures, in great dread trembling and quaking for meekness of joy, marvelling at the greatness of God the Maker and at the littleness of all that is made. For the beholding of this maketh the creature marvellously meek and mild.

Wherefore God willeth—and also it belongeth to us, both in nature and grace—that we wit and know of this, desiring this sight and this working; for it leadeth us in right way, and keepeth us in true life, and oneth us to God. And as good as God is, so great He is; and as much as it belongeth to His goodness to be loved, so much it belongeth to His greatness to be dreaded. For this reverent dread is the fair courtesy that is in Heaven afore God's face. And as much as He shall then be known and loved overpassing that He is now, in so much He shall be dreaded overpassing that He is now. Wherefore it behoveth needs to be that all Heaven and earth shall tremble and quake when the pillars shall tremble and quake.

CHAPTER LXXVI

"The soul that beholdeth the fair nature of our Lord Jesus, it hateth no hell but sin"

I speak but little of reverent dread, for I hope it may be seen in this matter aforesaid. But well I wot our Lord shewed me no souls but those that dread Him. For well I wot the soul that truly taketh the teaching of the Holy Ghost, it hateth more sin for vileness and horribleness than it doth all the pain that is in hell. For the soul that beholdeth the fair nature of our Lord Jesus, it hateth no hell but sin, as to my sight. And therefore it is God's will that we know sin, and pray busily and travail earnestly and seek teaching meekly that we fall not blindly therein; and if we fall, that we rise readily. For it is the most pain that the soul may have, to turn from God any time by sin.

The soul that willeth to be in rest when [an] other man's sin cometh to mind, he shall flee it as the pain of hell, seeking unto God for remedy, for help against it. For the beholding of other man's sins, it maketh as it were a thick mist afore the eyes of the soul, and we cannot, for the time, see the fairness of God, but if we may behold them with contrition with him, with compassion on him, and with holy desire to God for him. For without this it harmeth and tempesteth and hindereth the soul that beholdeth them. For this I understood in the Shewing of Compassion.

In this blissful Shewing of our Lord I have understanding of two contrary things: the one is the most wisdom that any creature may do in this life, the other is the most folly. The most wisdom is for a creature to do after the will and counsel of his highest sovereign Friend. This blessed Friend is Jesus, and it is His will and His counsel that we hold us with Him, and fasten us to Him homely—evermore, in what state soever that we be; for whether-so that we be foul or clean, we are all one in His loving. For weal nor for woe He willeth never we flee from Him. But because of the changeability that we are in, in our self, we fall often into sin. Then we have this [doubting dread] by the stirring of our enemy and by our own folly and blindness: for they say thus: *Thou seest well thou art a wretched creature, a sinner, and also unfaithful. For thou keepest not the Command; thou dost promise oftentimes our Lord that thou shalt do better, and anon after, thou fallest again into the same, especially into sloth and losing of time.* (For that is the beginning of sin, as to my sight,—and especially to the creatures that have given them to serve our Lord with inward beholding of His blessed Goodness.) And this maketh us adread to appear afore our courteous Lord. Thus is it our enemy that would put us aback with his false dread, [by reason] of our wretchedness, through pain that he threateth us with. For it is his meaning to make us so heavy and so weary in this, that we should let out of mind the fair, Blissful Beholding of our Everlasting Friend.

CHAPTER LXXVII

"Accuse not thyself overmuch, deeming that thy tribulation and thy woe is all thy fault." "All thy living is penance profitable." "In the remedy He willeth that we rejoice"

Our good Lord shewed the enmity of the Fiend: in which Shewing I understood that all that is contrary to love and peace is of the Fiend and of his part. And we have, of our feebleness and our folly, to fall; and we have, of mercy and grace of the Holy Ghost, to rise to more joy. And if our enemy aught winneth of us by our falling, (for it is his pleasure,) he loseth manifold more in our rising by charity and meekness. And this glorious rising, it is to him so great sorrow and pain for the hate that he hath to our soul, that he burneth continually in envy. And all this sorrow that he would make us to have, it shall turn to himself. And for this it was that our Lord scorned him, and [it was] this [that] made me mightily to laugh.

Then is this the remedy, that we be aware of our wretchedness and flee to our Lord: for ever the more needy that we be, the more speedful it is to us to draw nigh to Him. And let us say thus in our thinking: *I know well I have a shrewd pain; but our Lord is All-Mighty and may punish me mightily; and He is All-Wisdom and can punish me discerningly; and He is All-Goodness and loveth me full tenderly.* And in this beholding it is necessary for us to abide; for it is a lovely meekness of a sinful soul, wrought by mercy and grace of the Holy Ghost, when we willingly and gladly take the scourge and chastening of our Lord that Himself will give us. And it shall be full tender and full easy, if that we will only hold us satisfied with Him and with all His works.

For the penance that man taketh of himself was not shewed me: that is to say, it was not shewed specified. But specially and highly and with full lovely manner of look was it shewed that we shall meekly bear and suffer the penance that God Himself giveth us, with mind in His blessed Passion. (For when we have mind in His blessed Passion, with pity and love, then we suffer with Him like as His friends did that saw it. And this was shewed in the Thirteenth Shewing, near the beginning, where it speaketh of Pity.) For He saith: *Accuse not [thy]self overdone much, deeming that thy tribulation and thy woe is all for thy fault; for I will not that thou be heavy or sorrowful indiscreetly. For I tell thee, howsoever thou do, thou shalt have woe. And therefore I will that thou wisely know thy penance; and [thou] shalt see in truth that all thy living is penance profitable.*

This place is prison and this life is penance, and in the remedy He willeth that we rejoice. The remedy is that our Lord is with us, keeping and leading into the fulness of joy. For this is an endless joy to us in our Lord's signifying, that He that shall be our bliss when we are there, He is our keeper while we are here. Our way and our heaven is true love and sure trust; and of this He gave understanding in all [the Shewings] and especially in the Shewing of the Passion where He made me mightily to choose Him for my heaven.

Flee we to our Lord and we shall be comforted, touch we Him and we shall be made clean, cleave we to Him and we shall be sure, and safe from all manner of peril.

For our courteous Lord willeth that we should be as homely with Him as heart may think or soul may desire. But [let us] beware that we take not so recklessly this homeliness as to leave courtesy. For our Lord Himself is sovereign homeliness, and as homely as He is, so courteous He is: for He is very courteous. And the blessed creatures that shall be in heaven with Him without end, He will have them like to Himself in all things. And to be like our Lord perfectly, it is our very salvation and our full bliss.

And if we wot not how we shall do all this, desire we of our Lord and He shall teach us: for it is His own good-pleasure and His worship; blessed may He be!

CHAPTER LXXVIII

"Though we be highly lifted up into contemplation by the special gift of our Lord, yet it is needful to us to have knowledge and sight of our sin and our feebleness"

Our Lord of His mercy sheweth us our sin and our feebleness by the sweet gracious light of Himself; for our sin is so vile and so horrible that He of His courtesy will not shew it to us but by the light of His grace and mercy. Of four things therefore it is His will that we have knowing: the first is, that He is our Ground from whom we have all our life and our being. The second is, that He keepeth us mightily and mercifully in the time that we are in our sin and among all our enemies, that are full fell upon us; and so much we are in the more peril for [that] we give them occasion thereto, and know not our own need. The third is, how courteously He keepeth us, and *maketh us to know* that we go amiss. The fourth is, how steadfastly He abideth us and changeth no regard: for He willeth that we be turned [again], and oned to Him in love as He is to us.

And thus by this gracious knowing we may see our sin profitably without despair. For truly we need to see it, and by the sight we shall be made ashamed of our self and brought down as anent our pride and presumption; for it behoveth us verily to see that of ourselves we are right nought but sin and wretchedness. And thus by the sight of the less that our Lord sheweth us, the more is reckoned which we see not. For He of His courtesy measureth the sight to us; for it is so vile and so horrible that we should not endure to see it as it is. And by this meek knowing after this manner, through contrition and grace we shall be broken from all that is not our Lord. And then shall our blessed Saviour perfectly heal us, and one us to Him.

This breaking and this healing our Lord meaneth for the general Man. For he that is highest and nearest with God, he may see himself sinful—and needeth to—with me; and I that am the least and lowest that shall be saved, I may be comforted with him that is highest: so hath our Lord oned us in charity; [as] where He shewed me that I should sin.

And for joy that I had in beholding of Him I attended not readily to that Shewing, and our courteous Lord stopped there and would not further teach me till that He gave me grace and will to attend. And hereby was I learned that though we be highly lifted up into contemplation by the special gift of our Lord, yet it is needful to us therewith to have knowing and sight of our sin and our feebleness. For without this knowing we may not have true meekness, and without this [meekness] we may not be saved.

And afterward, also, I saw that we may not have this knowing from our self; nor from none of all our spiritual enemies: for they will us not so great good. For if it were by their will, we should not see it until our ending day. Then be we greatly beholden to God for that He will Himself, for love, shew it to us in time of mercy and grace.

CHAPTER LXXIX

"I was taught that I should see mine own sin, and not other men's sin except it may be for comfort and help of my fellow-Christians" ()

Also I had of this [Revelation] more understanding. In that He shewed me that I should sin, I took it nakedly to mine own singular person, for I was none otherwise shewed at that time. But by the high, gracious comfort of our Lord that followed after, I saw that His meaning was for the general Man: that is to say, All-Man; which is sinful and shall be unto the last day. Of which Man I am a member, as I hope, by the mercy of God. For the blessed comfort that I saw, it is large enough for us all. And here was I learned that I should see mine own sin, and not other men's sins but if it may be for comfort and help of mine even-Christians.

And also in this same Shewing where I saw that I should sin, there was I learned to be in dread for unsureness of myself. For I wot not how I shall fall, nor I know not the measure nor the greatness of sin; for that would I have wist, with dread, and thereto I had none answer.

Also our courteous Lord in the same time He shewed full surely and mightily the endlessness and the unchangeability of His love; and, afterward, that by His great goodness and His grace inwardly keeping, the love of Him and our soul shall never be disparted in two, without end.

And thus in this dread I have matter of meekness that saveth me from presumption, and in the blessed Shewing of Love I have matter of true comfort and of joy that saveth me from despair. All this homely Shewing of our courteous Lord, it is a lovely lesson and a sweet, gracious teaching of Himself in comforting of our soul. For He willeth that we [should] know by the sweetness and homely loving of Him, that all that we see or feel, within or without, that is contrary to this is of the enemy and not of God. And thus;—If we be stirred to be the more reckless of our living or of the keeping of our hearts because that we have knowing of this plenteous love, then need we greatly to beware. For this stirring, if it come, is untrue; and greatly we ought to hate it, for it all hath no likeness of God's will. And when that we be fallen, by frailty or blindness, then our courteous Lord toucheth us and stirreth us and calleth us; and then willeth He that we see our wretchedness and meekly be aware of it. But He willeth not that we abide thus, nor He willeth not that we busy us greatly about our accusing, nor He willeth not that we be wretched over our self; but He willeth that we hastily turn ourselves unto Him. For He standeth all aloof and abideth us sorrowfully and mournfully till when we come, and hath haste to have us to Him. For we are His joy and His delight, and He is our salve and our life.

When I say He standeth all alone, I leave the speaking of the blessed Company of heaven, and speak of His office and His working here on earth,—upon the condition of the Shewing.

CHAPTER LXXX

"Himself is nearest and meekest, highest and lowest, and doeth all."
"Love suffereth never to be without Pity"

By three things man standeth in this life; by which three God is worshipped, and we be speeded, kept and saved.

The first is, use of man's Reason natural; the second is, common teaching of Holy Church; the third is, inward gracious working of the Holy Ghost. And these three be all of one God: God is the ground of our natural reason; and God, the teaching of Holy Church; and God is the Holy Ghost. And all be sundry gifts to which He willeth that we have great regard, and attend us thereto. For these work in us continually all together; and these be great things. Of which great things He willeth that we have knowing here as it were in an A.B.C., that is to say, that we have a little knowing; whereof we shall have fulness in Heaven. And that is for to speed us.

We know in our Faith that God alone took our nature, and none but He; and furthermore that Christ alone did all the works that belong to our salvation, and none but He; and right so He alone doeth now the last end: that is to say, He dwelleth here with us, and ruleth us and governeth us in this living, and bringeth us to His bliss. And this shall He do as long as any soul is in earth that shall come to heaven,—and so far forth that if there were no such soul but one, He should be withal alone till He had brought him up to His bliss. I believe and understand the ministration of angels, as clerks tell us: but it was not shewed me. For Himself is nearest and meekest, highest and lowest, and doeth all. And not only all that we need, but also He doeth all that is worshipful, to our joy in heaven.

And where I say that He abideth sorrowfully and moaning, it meaneth all the true feeling that *we* have in our self, in contrition and compassion, and all sorrowing and moaning that we are not oned with our Lord. And all such that is speedful, it is Christ in us. And though some of us feel it seldom, it passeth never from Christ till what time He hath brought us out of all our woe. For love suffereth never to be without pity. And what time that we fall into sin and leave the mind of Him and the keeping of our own soul, then keepeth Christ alone all the charge; and thus standeth He sorrowfully and moaning.

Then belongeth it to us for reverence and kindness to turn us hastily to our Lord and leave Him not alone. He is here alone with us all: that is to say, only for us He is here. And what time I am strange to Him by sin, despair or sloth, then I let my Lord stand alone, in as much as it is in me. And thus it fareth with us all which be sinners. But though it be so that we do thus oftentimes, His Goodness suffereth us never to be alone, but lastingly He is with us, and tenderly He excuseth us, and ever shieldeth us from blame in His sight.

CHAPTER LXXXI

"God seeth all our living a penance: for nature-longing of our love is to Him a lasting penance in us." "His love maketh Him to long"

Our Good Lord shewed Himself in diverse manners both in heaven and in earth, but I saw Him take no place save in man's soul.

He shewed Himself in earth in the sweet Incarnation and in His blessed Passion. And in other manner He shewed Himself in earth [as in the Revelation] where I say: *I saw God in a Point.* And in another manner He shewed Himself in earth thus as it were in pilgrimage: that is to say, He is here with us, leading us, and shall be till when He hath brought us all to His bliss in heaven. He shewed Himself diverse times reigning, as it is aforesaid; but principally in man's soul. He hath taken there His resting-place and His worshipful City: out of which worshipful See He shall never rise nor remove without end.

Marvellous and stately is the place where the Lord dwelleth, and therefore He willeth that we readily answer to His gracious touching, more rejoicing in His whole love than sorrowing in our often fallings. For it is the most worship to Him of anything that we may do, that we live gladly and merrily, for His love, in our penance. For He beholdeth us so tenderly that He seeth all our living [here] a penance: for nature's longing in us is to Him aye-lasting penance in us: which penance He worketh in us and mercifully He helpeth us to bear it. For His love maketh *Him* to long [for us]; His wisdom and His truth with His rightfulness maketh *Him* to suffer us [to be] here: and in this same manner [of longing and abiding] He willeth to see it in us. For this is our natural penance,—and the highest, as to my sight. For this penance goeth never from us till what time that we be fulfilled, when we shall have Him to our meed. And therefore He willeth that we set our hearts in the Overpassing: that is to say, from the pain that we feel into the bliss that we trust.

CHAPTER LXXXII

"In falling and in rising we are ever preciously kept in one Love"

But here shewed our courteous Lord the moaning and the mourning of the soul, signifying thus: *I know well thou wilt live for my love, joyously and gladly suffering all the penance that may come to thee; but in as much as thou livest not without sin thou wouldest suffer, for my love, all the woe, all the tribulation and distress that might come to thee. And it is sooth. But be not greatly aggrieved with sin that falleth to thee against thy will.*

And here I understood that [which was shewed] that the Lord beholdeth the servant with pity and not with blame. For this passing life asketh not to live all without blame and sin. He loveth us endlessly, and we sin customably, and He sheweth us full mildly, and then we sorrow and mourn discreetly, turning us unto the beholding of His mercy, cleaving to His love and goodness, seeing that He is our medicine, perceiving that we do nought but sin. And thus by the meekness we get by the sight of our sin, faithfully knowing His everlasting love, Him thanking and praising, we please Him:—*I love thee, and thou lovest me, and our love shall not be disparted in two: for thy profit I suffer [these things to come].* And all this was shewed in spiritual understanding, saying these blessed words: *I keep thee full surely.*

And by the great desire that I saw in our blessed Lord that we shall live in this manner,—that is to say, in longing and enjoying, as all this lesson of love sheweth,—thereby I understood that that which is contrarious to us is not of Him but of enmity; and He willeth that we know it by the sweet gracious light of His kind love. If any such lover be in earth which is continually kept from falling, I know it not: for it was not shewed me. But this was shewed: that in falling and in rising we are ever preciously kept in one Love. For in the Beholding of God we fall not, and in the beholding of self we stand not; and both these [manners of beholding] be sooth as to my sight. But the Beholding of our Lord God is the highest soothness. Then are we greatly bound to God [for] that He willeth in this living to shew us this high soothness.

And I understood that while we be in this life it is full speedful to us that we see both these at once. For the higher Beholding keepeth us in spiritual solace and true enjoying in God; [and] that other that is the lower Beholding keepeth us in dread and maketh us ashamed of ourself. But our good Lord willeth ever that we hold us much more in the Beholding of the higher, and [yet] leave not the knowing of the lower, unto the time that we be brought up above, where we shall have our Lord Jesus unto our meed and be fulfilled of joy and bliss without end.

CHAPTER LXXXIII

"Life, Love, and Light"

I had, in part, touching, sight, and feeling in three properties of God, in which the strength and effect of all the Revelation standeth: and they were seen in every Shewing, and most properly in the Twelfth, where it saith oftentimes: [*It is I.*] The properties are these: Life, Love, and Light. In life is marvellous homeliness, and in love is gentle courtesy, and in light is endless Nature-hood. These properties were in one Goodness: unto which Goodness my Reason would be oned, and cleave to it with all its might.

I beheld with reverent dread, and highly marvelling in the sight and in the feeling of the sweet accord, that our Reason is in God; understanding that it is the highest gift that we have received; and it is grounded in nature.

Our faith is a light by nature coming of our endless Day, that is our Father, God. In which light our Mother, Christ, and our good Lord, the Holy Ghost, leadeth us in this passing life. This light is measured discreetly, needfully standing to us in the night. The light is cause of our life; the night is cause of our pain and of all our woe: in which we earn meed and thanks of God. For we, with mercy and grace, steadfastly know and believe our light, going therein wisely and mightily.

And at the end of woe, suddenly our eyes shall be opened, and in clearness of light our sight shall be full: which light is God, our Maker and Holy Ghost, in Christ Jesus our Saviour.

Thus I saw and understood that our faith is our light in our night: which light is God, our endless Day.

CHAPTER LXXXIV

"Charity"

The light is Charity, and the measuring of this light is done to us profitably by the wisdom of God. For neither is the light so large that we may see our blissful Day, nor is it shut from us; but it is such a light in which we may live meedfully, with travail deserving the endless worship of God. And this was seen in the Sixth Shewing where He said: *I thank thee of thy service and of thy travail*. Thus Charity keepeth us in Faith and Hope, and Hope leadeth us in Charity. And in the end all shall be Charity.

I had three manners of understanding of this light, Charity. The first is Charity unmade; the second is Charity made; the third is Charity given. Charity unmade is God; Charity made is our soul in God; Charity given is virtue. And that is a precious gift of working in which we love God, for Himself; and ourselves, in God; and that which God loveth, for God.

CHAPTER LXXXV

"Lord, blessed mayest Thou be, for it is thus: it is well"

And in this sight I marvelled highly. For notwithstanding our simple living and our blindness here, yet endlessly our courteous Lord beholdeth us in this working, rejoicing; and of all things, we may please Him best wisely and truly to believe, and to enjoy with Him and in Him. For as verily as we shall be in the bliss of God without end, Him praising and thanking, so verily we have been in the foresight of God, loved and known in His endless purpose from without beginning. In which unbegun love He made us; and in the same love He keepeth us and never suffereth us to be hurt [in manner] by which our bliss might be lost. And therefore when the Doom is given and we be all brought up above, then shall we clearly see in God the secret things which be now hid to us. Then shall none of us be stirred to say in any wise: *Lord, if it had been thus, then it had been full well*; but we shall say all with one voice: *Lord, blessed mayst thou be, for it is thus: it is well; and now see we verily that all-thing is done as it was then ordained before that anything was made.*

CHAPTER LXXXVI

"Love was our Lord's Meaning"

This book is begun by God's gift and His grace, but it is not yet performed, as to my sight.

For Charity pray we all; [together] with *God's* working, thanking, trusting, enjoying. For thus will our good Lord be prayed to, as by the understanding that I took of all His own meaning and of the sweet words where He saith full merrily: *I am the Ground of thy beseeching.* For truly I saw and understood in our Lord's meaning that He shewed it for that He willeth to have it known more than it is: in which knowing He will give us grace to love to Him and cleave to Him. For He beholdeth His heavenly treasure with so great love on earth that He willeth to give us more light and solace in heavenly joy, in drawing to Him of our hearts, for sorrow and darkness which we are in.

And from that time that it was shewed I desired oftentimes to learn what was our Lord's meaning. And fifteen years after, and more, I was answered in ghostly understanding, saying thus: *Wouldst thou learn thy Lord's meaning in this thing? Learn it well: Love was His meaning. Who shewed it thee? Love. What shewed He thee? Love. Wherefore shewed it He? For Love. Hold thee therein and thou shalt learn and know more in the same. But thou shalt never know nor learn therein other thing without end.* Thus was I learned that Love was our Lord's meaning.

And I saw full surely that ere God made us He loved us; which love was never slacked, nor ever shall be. And in this love He hath done all His works; and in this love He hath made all things profitable to us; and in this love our life is everlasting. In our making we had beginning; but the love wherein He made us was in Him from without beginning: in which love we have our beginning. And all this shall we see in God, without end.

POSTSCRIPT BY A SCRIBE

Which Jesus mot grant us

Amen.

[And to him also may be assigned this conclusion:—]

Thus endeth the Revelation of Love of the blissid Trinite shewid by our Savior Christ Jesu for our endles comfort and solace and also to enjoyen in him in this passand journey of this life.

Amen Jesu Amen

I pray Almyty God that this booke com not but to the hands of them that will be his faithfull lovers, and to those that will submitt them to the faith of holy Church, and obey the holesom understondying and teching of the men that be of vertuous life, sadde Age and sound lering: ffor this Revelation is hey Divinitye and hey wisdom, wherfore it may not dwelle with him that is thrall to synne and to the Devill.

And beware thou take not on thing after thy affection and liking, and leve another: for that is the condition of an heretique. But take every thing with other. And, trewly understonden, All is according to holy Scripture and groundid in the same. And *that* Jesus, our very love, light and truth, shall shew to all clen soulis that with mekeness aske profe reverently this wisdom of hym.

And thou to whom this boke shall come, thank heyley and hertily our Saviour Christ Jesu that he made these shewings and revelations, for the, and to the, of his endles love, mercy and goodnes for thine and our save guide, to conduct to everlastying bliss: *the which Jesus mot grant us.* Amen.